DIRECT SALES

Done Right

DIRECT SALES

Done Right

A Proven Path to Stop Wasting Time & Start Making **MEANINGFUL** Money

Katy Ursta

PUBLISHED BY *Chic* INFLUENCER USA, 2023

*For my boys, the ones God blessed me to
do life with, Mike, Nick, and Dom.*

COME SAY *Hi*

I CAN'T WAIT TO MEET YOU!

 Katy Ursta
Chic Influencer

 @katywritescontent
@chicinfluencer

 support@chicinfluencer.com

DIRECT SALES DONE RIGHT *Academy*

In this online self-paced academy, you will go from being overwhelmed, unorganized, and anxious about the steps to success in your direct sales business to being organized, empowered, and clear on how to confidently achieve your direct sales goals.

- <u>5 core lessons</u> to build a successful direct sales business
- 5 pre-recorded <u>Q+A sessions</u>
- <u>Lifetime access</u> to recordings and resources
- <u>Comprehensive workbook</u> to guide you through the course

Created by Direct Sales experts, Melanie Mitro and Katy Ursta.

Learn more!

DIRECT SALES DONE RIGHT ACADEMY *Testimonials*

RACHEL S.

Absolute consistency has gotten me to the next rank. My PV/GV over the last three months has been consistently higher than before the course and focusing on specific actions.

I would (and have) recommended this course to anyone in direct sales. It opened my eyes to practices I would not have thought to try on my own and it has helped me see where I was lacking in my business and practices and what I needed to do to get things on track to success!

EDWINA K.

You always hear, identify your ideal client. But until the Direct Sales Done Right Academy, I didn't feel I had a step-by-step roadmap for clearly defining who that is. Now that I took this course, I clearly understand who I want to work with, who I best serve and how social media is the vehicle for connecting with her.

MISSY F.

I just came back from our 2nd annual convention with 3 awards! I was so happy! I ranked 3rd place in top personal sales volume, and won the vendor of the year award and the spirit of Topanga award. What a great year! I could not have done it without all of your help. You guys have helped me more than you know!

Your one-stop shop for building a successful direct sales business.

Direct Sales Done *Right* Podcast

Hosted By

Melanie Mitro + Katy Ursta

A new episode
every Thursday!

Listen Here!

DIRECT SALES DONE RIGHT *Planner*

Learn more!

The Direct Sales Done Right 52 Week Business and Marketing Planner teaches you 4 systems to creating a business and life that you love, without the burnout.

TABLE OF *Contents*

TABLE OF *Contents*

FOREWORD

When I had my first baby, I got the book *What To Expect When Expecting*. After reading it, I felt like I was going to be well prepared for motherhood, only to realize that the book left out all of the emotional ups and downs and the dark side of what motherhood is truly like. I felt lied to and like someone needed to write a tell-all, no-holds-barred book about what you actually go through when having a baby. You know, something that really explained what it was like to endure labor, or trying to get your infant to latch, or surviving sleepless nights for weeks on end, or the mom-guilt that comes from struggling to love the "job" of motherhood as much as you love your kids.

Now, I'm sure you're asking yourself how this relates to *Direct Sales Done Right*. While the famous baby book glossed over important (and sometimes painful) details, *Direct Sales Done Right* tells it all—the good, the bad, and the gritty. This book is perfect for any woman in direct sales who needs a clear and radically honest roadmap to achieve direct sales success. If you are looking for someone to shoot straight on what it takes to achieve the desires in your heart, this is the perfect place to start. There are so many experts out there who skirt around the ups and downs you will face while building your business, but this book holds nothing back.

Katy's approach is honest and thoughtful. Direct sales isn't all rainbows and butterflies. Building a business isn't a walk in the park. Seeing the full scope of what you can expect throughout your journey is going to help prepare you and also provide comfort that you are not alone. You will walk away with a complete overview of the mindset, strategy, and considerations needed to take the next steps in your direct sales success. When you put the work in, you truly can have a thriving direct sales business and a healthy personal life. No matter where you are in your direct sales journey, the lessons in this book are going to help you get from where you are today to where you want to go. Katy provides a transparent, step-by-step roadmap of what it takes to get the business off the ground and become profitable ASAP.

I met Katy in 2003 when she was pledging our sorority, Alpha Sigma Alpha. It wasn't until nine years later that we reconnected when she joined my direct sales team. After watching me share my love for fitness and the business on social media, she decided it could be a great opportunity to make a little extra income to make life more comfortable.

She signed up and immediately booked a party with the neighbors to kick off the business. We showed up with product samples, pamphlets, and lots of energy, even though we both had no idea what we were doing! I watched Katy build her business in between teaching and parenting. She was so good at managing her time and being smart about how she showed up in the pockets of her day to hit her goals.

She grew her customer base and team quickly, advancing to the top .01% of the company the following year. Because of her hard work and discipline, she was able to take extended maternity leave when she had her second child. During her maternity leave, she was diagnosed with Stage 4 Hodgkins Lymphoma. I will never forget Katy coming over to my house where we sat at the desk in my basement and talked about how we would figure this out. I told her she wouldn't have to do any of this alone.

In the next few years, Katy went on to see massive growth in her team, achieved the Humanitarian Award in our company, and raised over seventy thousand dollars for the Leukemia and Lymphoma Society.

She truly created a movement within our organization that was tied to so much more than a workout and our products. She was sweating for something more! She was giving other people prayer and support when they needed it most.

Over the past eleven years of working together in our direct sales business, we have run training and push groups, team calls, live events, and launched the business internationally. We have grown together as friends and as co-owners of our company, Chic Influencer, which provides courses, community, membership, and private coaching to women in direct sales.

What I love most about Katy is that she is very detail-oriented and always analyzes decisions before we jump into action. She is excellent at customer service and creating a unique experience for any customer that comes through our doors. She can move people to tears with her powerful stories and truly get people to dig into the why behind what they do as direct sellers.

Katy has taught me to set healthy boundaries and prioritize joy, which, as an Enneagram 3, is not easy for me!

I am so excited for you to read *Direct Sales Done Right* because I know how you are feeling right now. You feel like you should be further along than you are. You feel like success isn't happening fast enough. You are maybe even questioning whether or not you are cut out for success. What are people going to think if I pursue a non-traditional career path? Katy has walked the walk and talked the talk, and she is about to bust every self-limiting belief you have about success and then arm you with the tools to navigate through the messy middle of building your dream life. The one thing I always look for in a mentor is someone who has already done what I want to do so they can guide me through the journey. That is Katy! She is your go-to girl when it comes to building a business that makes you feel great and also creates a significant income.

Now let's dig in and get started with the process of transforming your life and business. Are you ready?!

Sincerely,

Melanie Mitro

@melaniemitro on IG

INTRODUCTION

"When you know better, you do better."

- EVERYONE WHO HAS FAILED OR FLOPPED
THEIR WAY TO SUCCESS

O h, friend! I am so glad that you are here, and as much as I would love to be sitting right next to you in the trenches of your living room, or office, or heck, even your car, while you are building your direct sales business, I suppose this book is going to have to do.

I need to ask, do you realize how fortunate you are to be part of an industry that doesn't cap potential? In this industry you have the potential to create a life others can only dream of. Travel, growth, flexibility, and income; all of it is possible through this industry.

And because we are going to be spending a lot of time together, I need you to know something.

This business model has changed the trajectory of my life. As a classroom teacher who once refused to read personal development because it was not part of my contractual obligations (I actually stormed into the principal's office with Stephen Covey's *7 Habits of Highly Effective People*, threw it on his desk and said, "You can't make us read this." Not my finest hour, but more on that in the coming chapter), I am happy to report that the very same book which I vehemently refused to read has become a foundation of my professional and personal life.

Let me be clear though, I haven't always gotten it right. Direct sales, I mean. I haven't always nailed it.

If I could go back to the beginning, I think I would do things differently. Not in a regretful way, but in an educated way. Over the past eleven years of working in the industry, I've learned a thing or two about building a direct sales business, and since we're going to be spending some time together, I think it's important to be transparent and let you know that I've made some mistakes along the way.

Here are a few of the things I've gotten really wrong (I'd like to think that if we were sitting together having a cup of coffee, you would be shaking your head "yes" to a few of these as well).

Direct Sales less than shining moments:
- I've fallen into the trap of comparison.

- I've prioritized a paycheck over people.
- I've fallen into the "hustle more" mentality.
- I've overthought just about everything.
- I've been inconsistent with action.
- I've posted from a place of desperation.
- I've sent the cringeworthy, "Hey girl!" messages.
- I've made decisions that served my goals instead of my community.
- I've lost sight of my priorities.
- I've come off as *that network marketer.*

And yet, here I am with a decade-plus of experience in the direct sales industry, successfully continuing to learn and grow (while still failing forward).

I want to make myself abundantly clear. Every failure I share throughout the book started with good intentions, I just had to learn a better way. And friend, I am here to teach you a better way of doing direct sales.

Here's What They Aren't Telling You About the Industry

Before we dig in too far, let's bring a little clarity. Throughout the text, I will refer to the industry as direct sales. However, there are many similarities between direct sales and network marketing. Whether you are in direct sales or network marketing, the tools mentioned within the book will support your goals! Here's a quick reference to learn more about each model:

In a direct sales business, the focus is primarily on product sales over recruitment (onboarding new distributors). Direct sales typically pay higher commissions. In multi-level marketing (MLM), also referred to as network marketing, you earn commissions on what you sell and directly by recruiting people. You earn a commission on your team's sales, too.

According to a recent study, in 2020, the number of people using the direct sales model to sell products or services broke records with 7.7 million—a 13.2 percent increase over 2019—and with 41.6 million enjoying the discount through preferred customer and discount buyer opportunities. The report also revealed that 77 percent of Americans are interested in flexible, entrepreneurial opportunities, with 91 percent of Gen Z and 88 percent of Millennials showing interest in direct selling.

What's even more incredible is that the study revealed a growing shift to purchasing online from direct sellers, and 46% of those participating in the survey are *willing to welcome contact from direct sellers regarding business opportunities on social media.*[1]

The good news is the narrative surrounding the often misunderstood business model is changing which means that more women (and men too) are seeing direct sales as a viable income stream because *it is!*

To play devil's advocate though, many people within the industry give it a bad reputation. Let me assure you, coming off as one of *those network marketers* has never been my intention, and I'm sure it's not yours either. I've come to realize that there's a reason direct sales, more specifically direct sellers who are part of a network marketing opportunity, get a bad rep. It's because they just don't know the best way to approach the business. And in the beginning, I didn't help the reputation of the model much.

So, before we begin, can we clear the air, completely tabula rasa everything and forgive ourselves for our imperfect action? Can we forgive ourselves for the goals we've missed, the invitation that never got sent, and the mistakes we've made? Can we forgive ourselves for the times we took the wrong approach, sent mass messages, and started conversations with strangers with the words "hey girl?" (I know. I am cringing, too).

Every single one of the experiences that you've had so far brought you here to this book. Even if that experience is, "I just signed up and I have no idea what I am doing!" What you do moving forward is entirely up to you. From here on out, this is where it counts.

I've learned to do better through a lot of mistakes, terrible marketing fails, and missed goals. I speak from a place of understanding. My goal over the following chapters, and likely a large amount of coffee, is to help you see a better way, to help you do *Direct Sales Done Right.*

This book is a compilation of over a decade of personal experience—eleven years of highs and lows, of learning, growing, and evolving.

My goal is to help you take ownership of your direct sales (or network market-

---

1 DSJ Staff, "Attitudes toward Direct Selling: How Entrepreneurs and Consumers See the Channel," *Direct Selling Journal,* May 17, 2022, https://www.dsa.org/direct-selling-journal/direct-selling-journal-latest-articles/attitudes-toward-direct-selling-how-entrepreneurs-and-consumers-see-the-channel

ing) business, define your own terms of success, and confidently share the business opportunity with others using the tools and resources that helped me to scale in the industry.

I've read countless books, listened to hundreds of motivational speakers, and have a playlist of about 100 podcasts about building a direct sales business. While I've been able to pull nuggets of wisdom from my years of research, there is no better teacher than personal experience.

I won't be spending a lot of time talking about specific content to create on social media, because outside of this book, I've co-created *The Direct Sales Done Right Planner* to help you clarify your brand messaging and deliver marketing content to your ideal customers and team members. You will, however, find an entire business blueprint in this book to develop the foundation of a successful direct sales business—no specific skill set is required.

 Scan the QR code to learn more about *The Direct Sales Done Right Planner!*

I should probably tell you a little bit about me. I am a mom of two wild kiddos, Nick and Dom, and in this season of my life, I am spending an obscene amount of time at hockey rinks. Before starting in direct sales (and even in the early days of launching my business), I was a seventh-grade reading teacher. I met my husband, Mike, at a college bar and proclaimed to my sorority sister, "You see that guy over there? I am going to marry the sh*t out of him." It wasn't the classiest of phrases, but we've been married for sixteen years, and despite my vocal, somewhat crass proclamation, he's become my number one supporter and also the first to admit that if I want something, I make it happen. Who knows if he knew back then the wild ride he was getting into?

But eleven years ago, while Mike and I had great jobs where we were working hard, we found ourselves fighting over finances and wondering how anyone did more than just get by. When I discovered the direct sales opportunity, I was working just about every after-school extra curricular to bring home additional income, burying myself in all the personal development books I could get my hands on, and participating in every single direct sales training I heard of!

While working full-time with a young son and expecting our second child, I set a goal in direct sales to extend my maternity leave so I could be home longer once my second son arrived. Life threw a curveball my way when I was diagnosed with Stage 4 cancer during my extended maternity leave. Without the security of my income and healthcare benefits I got through teaching, I decided to lean into the direct sales business opportunity. That year, while undergoing rigorous chemotherapy, my business grew over 300%.

Cancer changes things, no doubt about that. But I believe it's up to us to decide how our struggles change us. Personally, cancer gave me this understanding of the brevity of time and God-honoring priorities. In fact, during the battle, my confidence grew around what the business allowed me to do: heal while going through treatment without the burden of financial struggle, spend more time with my family, and share a new perspective of movement and working out on a public platform. I thrived in the industry despite my sickness. On top of that, I started to speak without fear about the blessings of the business, the importance of sweating for something bigger than a few calories burned, and the pursuit of new ventures such as fundraising, speaking, and writing (one of my first publications, *The Back Pocket Prayer Journal*, is still available on Amazon). During that time, I didn't just grow my business 300%. I found my Unique Sharing Proposition, a term I will spend a lot of time exploring in Section Three. I took a different approach to the business than my peers, and it became a social media movement that I still see others implement today (Every. Sweat. Matters.)

 Scan the QR code to learn more about *The Back Pocket Prayer Journal!*

It's safe to say my life changed beautifully because of the battle and the business. And friend, I have no doubt it can do the same for you.

Throughout this book, I provide real-life examples of the times I got direct sales right and the times I got it wildly wrong. I truly believe that direct sales is an incredible profession. It allows you to design your own outcome based on your efforts. Want to travel the world? Direct sales can help with that. Homeschool your kids? Direct sales can help with that. Build a community of women who lift you up? Direct sales can help with that. Be able to give of your time and resources more freely? Direct sales can help with that. The opportunity in front of you, my friend, is endless, but there's a commitment on your part—a commitment to *Direct Sales Done Right*. Are you ready to dive in?

How to Use This Book

The book is divided into six essential sections that will help you develop skills while reflecting on your personal habits:

- The Mindset of a Successful Direct Seller: Not Just Another Lifehack
- Of Course It's Personal, It's Business: Owning Your Role in Success
- Serving Through Your Social Media: Your Winning Content Strategy
- The Healthy Pipeline: Creating the Ultimate Hype Squad
- Let's Not Make This Awkward: Having Conversations That Actually Close
- The Healthy CEO: Break In Case of Emergency

Each section will include a recap at the end of the biggest takeaways and my final thoughts that will help you implement the teachings immediately. As we say in the direct sales business often, "Imperfect action is better than perfect inaction." The more you implement the teachings immediately, the more likely you will be to create an impactful habit.

A note about the book:

Melanie Mitro, my business partner at Chic Influencer, as well as my personal direct sales upline (sponsor), is also a 4x top in industry leader with a downline of 10,000 and a person recruiting goal of 30+ at the prime of her business. If anyone knows anything about taking the right action, it's Melanie. I have brought her on to help in sharing stories and experiences that will illustrate the potential of this industry.

Direct Sales Done Right is your playbook to building a direct sales business with confidence and profitability. You will also find tucked into Section Five of the book helpful scripts for what to say when you're ready to extend the invite without sounding salesy. And if you're looking for laser-focused guidance on specific content to create on social media, head on over to chicinfluencer.com where you can access tons of trainings as well as *The Direct Sales Done Right Planner*.

Your *Direct Sales Done Right* Commitment

I'd like to say a few words, on the record, about my experience building a direct sales business. It wasn't always easy, most of it was messy, and to sugarcoat the experience would be a huge disservice to you. Full transparency is the only way to approach this book and the business. While direct sales is an imperfect business model, it can create an opportunity for anyone, but it isn't necessarily for everyone.

This book is your judgment-free zone, your, "Whoa. She went through this too. It's so good to know I am not alone," zone. No lies: I am somewhat mortified to share a few of my less-than-glittering stories of building a business, but each story is told with the intention to call you to action. After all, isn't that why you're here?

You know that having good intentions of building a business won't actually build the business, but you know action will. So, my promise is to guide you with the action steps and arm you with my personal mistakes to possibly save you from making a few of them yourself. Are you ready to make a commitment to doing *Direct Sales Done Right* and seeing it through?

Are you willing to make a few commitments to yourself as well? Are you willing to do the work that's less than Instaworthy? Are you willing to break up with the beliefs you have about the model and what you've heard from those who didn't see success in the industry? Are you willing to take action?

You need to know that success in direct sales *is possible* for you. You can build a business you love and create freedom beyond what you've ever been taught.

Is it easy? No. Is it possible? Absolutely. There is a right way to build a direct sales business. Are you ready?

I, _____, am committed to taking imperfect action (knowing it's better than perfect inaction) in my direct sales business _____ (name of company). I am willing to learn from my mistakes, celebrate my wins, share the experience with others along the way, and create my own definition of success.

Let's do this!

SIGN _____

Rooting for you every step of the way,
Katy

Section One

The Mindset of a Successful Direct Seller: Not Just Another Lifehack

"The truth is, the top-secret conversations you have in the privacy of your own mind do not stay confidential forever. These thoughts will eventually be revealed for everyone to see. A dream, a business, or a marriage dies first in the mind. Your best and worst decision began with an individual thought."

- TOMMY NEWBERRY, *40 DAYS TO A JOY-FILLED LIFE*

A few years ago, I attended a conference that provided an opportunity for the audience to "walk on fire" after hours of running on adrenaline fueled by the speakers and the spectacle taking place on the stage and within the stands. There was a different level of energy, a contagious feeling of taking on the world, a power over the possibility, and a crystal clear belief that anything was possible. So, like the thousands of others amped and armed with energy, I walked on hot coals, high-fiving everyone on the other side, and left that conference ready to bring serious heat to my business.

AND THEN…

When I got home, I was a little jet-lagged. My husband had been with the kids for days on his own and needed a break. There was so much laundry to do (a problem that, to this day, is never ending). And that fire within me soon turned to embers before burning out completely.

Sounds familiar, doesn't it? One minute you're on fire, the next minute you're Googling how to get motivated. I mean, how often do we feed the flames of possibility only to feel like the burn out is unavoidable?

Do you ever find yourself listening to company trainings or attending events and thinking, "NOW! YES! THIS IS IT! IT'S MY TIME," only to fall back into your old pattern? Only each time, you adopt a little more doubt, a little more resentment, or a little more fear? So, you delay taking action and replace it with compounding thoughts of "I can't."

In her book, *101 Essays That Will Change the Way You Think*, Brianna Wiest challenges readers to reclaim the way they look at fire. She states, "Fire can burn your house down, or it can cook you dinner each night and keep you warm in the winter. Your mind works the same way."[2]

Friend, the fire isn't the problem. Motivation isn't the problem. That fire in your business, the passion you have to build a direct sales business, can work for you or work against you. We don't need to put our focus on the fire. The problem is our mindset, the way you think about you. We need to focus on the mindset it takes to stoke the fire and keep it *steadily* glowing for the long haul.

How? First, we have to call out a simple truth. You, me, and everyone in between is hardwired to focus on the negative.

Fun fact: Did you know that we are hardwired to see the negative in life five times more than the positive? Fun fact: The negativity bias was wired into us to help us survive (ie. fire = hot, don't go out of the cave, you might die). Fun fact: When it comes to motivation, we're more likely to be motivated to change from a place of pain than from a place of pleasure. Okay, maybe not so fun facts, more like Debbie Downer facts…

But here's the *really* fun fact: In order to change, we actually have to break our thought patterns. Change doesn't start with action, it starts with thoughts. *We have to change our thought patterns in order to achieve results.* That goes for business. That goes for our fitness goals. That goes for relationships. That goes for any change you need or want to make.

If you want to change your relationship, it starts with your thoughts.
If you want to change your routine, it starts with your thoughts.
If you want to change your habits, it starts with your thoughts.
If you want to change your business, it starts with your thoughts.
If you want to change your life, it starts with your thoughts.

Here's the deal. There's no way to skirt around it anymore. We have to get right into what you think of yourself. I know, I know, right? "Just tell me what to do to be successful, Katy." I promise I will give you the formulas and the strategies, but before we do any of that, let's start with the question, "What do you really think of yourself?"

If your first thought is, "I've heard that before," or, "I don't need this personal

---

2 Brianna Wiest, *101 Essays That Will Change the Way You Think*, ebook edition, (Thought Catalogs Books, 2017).

development garbage," or, "That's not the real issue for me," or, "I've tried before," then I've got news for you. Your thought patterns are negative. Did you see? Did you see how easy that was to go straight to the negative?

Everything I teach in this book is going to force you to look at your current actions and your current thought patterns. They work together, it's kind of like a package deal.

Peanut butter and jelly. Cookies and milk. Jim and Pam. Tacos and Tuesdays.

Throughout Section One, we will explore the mindset of a successful direct seller. As I mentioned, we falsely believe that motivation is the problem. It's not. In fact, motivation can only take us so far. One of the biggest roadblocks in business is our current thought patterns and the need to replace them with new patterns.

Imagine that Chip and Joanna Gaines are all like, "Hey, we want to give you a full home renovation! You down?" And you're like, "Makeover?! Sure! It could use a little sprucing up!" Just as a house can become tired and in need of sprucing up, our minds can become bogged down by negative thoughts that hold us back!

So before you take a hammer to your home, let's start with the bones of your business: your mindset. We are going to lay down the structure for *Direct Sales Done Right* but not without talking about what goes on behind the scenes.

Just like in a home makeover, we will begin replacing a negative thought pattern, which means identifying those negative beliefs and thought processes that are dragging you down and replacing them with positive, empowering ones.

It's going to get messy! It may take some time and effort, just like a home renovation, but the end result is worth it. Imagine your mind as a beautiful, welcoming, and functional space that supports your goals and dreams. It's like a cozy and inviting house where you feel happy, confident, and fulfilled!

In this section we are going to cover:
- The Cave Mindset: Overcoming Your Limiting Beliefs
- The Belief Trifecta
- Vision Casting Done Right
- Act As If Statements

We have a lot of ground to cover in our mindset renovation, so grab your hard hat (or at least a cup of coffee) and a sledgehammer, because we're about to bring on the demolition of those limiting beliefs!

Chapter One

"Success is the progressive realization of a worthy goal or ideal. By this definition, success is not a destination but a journey. It's not something you acquire or achieve. It's something you become as you work towards your goals."

- STEPHEN COVEY, *THE 7 HABITS OF HIGHLY EFFECTIVE PEOPLE*

C an I be honest with you? Maybe you are like me, but when I went into direct sales, I had no idea what I was doing, and I certainly had no idea what it was going to take to reach my own version of success. That version of me who started in direct sales over ten years ago would've seen a quote like Stephen Covey's and rolled her eyes at the fluffiness of it all. Little did I know just how much my mindset would change throughout the process of building a business. Back then, I didn't know what I didn't know. I didn't know about the hours of work that lay ahead. I didn't know about the countless hours I'd spend inviting prospects to the opportunity, only to be rejected time and time again. I didn't know the vast number of people who would come into my life and, likewise, the people who would leave. I had no idea what it was really going to take to build a direct sales business, and I certainly didn't know who I would become through the process.

I don't say any of this to scare you. In fact, quite the opposite. Trust me, I take it very seriously that you invested in this book and are learning from my direct selling experience. So, before we dive into the mindset work it took to get where I am currently, I need to get this one thing off my chest…

We wildly underestimate what it's going to take to be successful. Not in a cheesy "destination versus journey" way, but in a "nose to the grindstone" kind of way. There's no getting around the work it's going to take to be successful (don't worry, I provide a roadmap within these pages to outline the necessary action steps). Let's also not skirt around this fact: The person you are today, the one building the business, is going to grow. The type of person you are becoming matters far more than the goals you are achieving, and if you are going to succeed in this business it will be impossible not to change. In order to succeed, you're going to evolve.

Want proof? I'm not proud of the story I am going to share, but since I am going to be guiding you over the coming chapters, I need to confess a little about the woman I was before I was introduced to the direct sales opportunity.

Long before I started in direct sales, I was teaching reading to middle schoolers. As a contracted teacher, my job role and responsibilities were my obligation. I was an employee. I was paid a salary to do a specific job, a job which I often brought home with me.

It's no secret that educators often go above and beyond the call of duty, spending evenings grading papers and early mornings before the bell rings with the kiddos. When there wasn't money left in the school budget for supplies, I frequently found myself at the craft store or Walmart®, making sure the students had access to everything they needed.

About one year before I started direct selling, the principal approached me and several other colleagues about participating in a required book study. We'd be using our own time to read Stephen Covey's *7 Habits of Highly Effective People*. It wasn't a book that I'd be teaching the kids; it had nothing to do with the curriculum. So, dumbfounded, I (along with my colleagues) responded with a very limited mindset. It was a hard, "No." Not in the contract. I didn't have time. And who did he think he was, telling me I should participate in a self-help book study? I remember tossing the book down on his desk and saying, "Sorry. It's not part of the contract."

My stomach turns in knots thinking about that time in my life—a time that was also punctuated by stacks of bills and the constant responsibility of keeping all the plates spinning in the air. I think about the stress of it all and my old mindset of *never enough*.

It was a time in my life when my husband and I were just getting by week to week. A time when mindset work was pointless nonsense. A time when dreaming big and my potential outside of my teaching job were non-existent, not even on my radar.

Although I never thought of myself as being trapped, I didn't have the clarity to see outside of my then-situation. Like so many before me, I didn't know what I didn't know. And maybe that's where you are right now? Maybe you've joined direct sales with the hopes of providing a better life for your family. Maybe you're curious about the possibility. But maybe, like me, you're also a little skeptical.

Wherever you are right now is exactly where you need to be. Whatever fears and uncertainties you have, we will unpack them together.

My limitations back then existed because I didn't personally know anyone entrepreneurial, and I certainly didn't have a belief (aside from winning the lottery) that I could do anything more than just get by.

To be clear, I really loved my job. I loved my students. I loved the work I got to do. But I didn't love the financial stress. I didn't love the grind of doing the same thing day in and day out, wondering if there was more to life than just getting by. Looking back, it's evident that I had a fixed mindset: I didn't really believe that my situation was within my control to change. In her book, *Mindset*, Carol Dweck describes the people who see qualities as fixed traits as those who don't believe that change is within their control. On the flip side, people with a growth mindset feel their skills and intelligence can be improved with effort and persistence.

Employee Mindset

- You wait for others to tell you what to do.
- You believe success comes from talent.
- You only do the bare minimum to get by.
- You only do what is in the job description.
- You avoid challenges.
- You get defensive or give up easily.
- You feel threatened by the success of others.

CEO Mindset

- You use Google and Youtube as a search bar.
- You are always listening to PD.
- You constantly ask if this is the best use of your time.
- You notice when you get complacent and find ways to reignite your fire.
- You embrace challenges.
- You persist in the face of setbacks.
- You find inspiration in others' success.
- You don't need someone to tell you what to do.
- You are constantly learning and growing.

Maybe you're looking at this chart realizing that your mindset, like mine, is fixed. Maybe you've seen others around you succeed and even cheered them on, but you don't actually think it's possible for yourself. Or maybe you've been dreaming big for a long time, but setbacks and failures seem to keep your thoughts captive. Maybe you just think you're past your prime. Maybe you know you're stuck but you don't know why. Sound all too familiar?

Maybe, just maybe, you are stuck in what I call the Cave Mindset. But, as promised, I am going to give you the tools to break out of the fixed mindset into the growth mindset!

The Cave Mindset

You've probably heard of Plato, but if you're struggling to remember why he's important, he was a famous philosopher who lived from c. 428-347 B.C., and he was *really good* at challenging people to view the world differently. He helped shape cultural expectations and beliefs about government, truth, reality, and even moral issues that still persist today. In a nutshell, he changed the way we thought about thinking.

One of Plato's most famous works is known as *The Allegory of the Cave*. In it, he described three prisoners in a cave who had forever been chained by their feet, doomed for eternity to stare at a wall that illuminated the shadows of what was happening in the world behind them. The shadows on the wall in front of the prisoners were the *only* reality they'd ever known or seen.

One day, one of the prisoners breaks free. He turns around, recognizing that the shadows in front of him were not reality, only a small picture of what had actually been happening behind him. The whole time he was chained inside the cave, outside there was a world of color, vibrancy, movement, and vastness.

He runs back into the cave to tell the other prisoners and set them free so that they, too, can experience the richness of the world outside the cave.

But to his disappointment, the chained prisoners shame him. They want nothing to do with life outside the cave. They mock the free man for his crazy ideas. They refuse to believe what they don't understand.

Layered within Plato's allegory is a simple truth that I often carry with me and that has served me throughout my years of business in direct sales:

Some will.

Some won't.

Someone is waiting.

Keep going.

Gosh, Katy-before-direct-sales, she related to those captives in the cave. I knew that having a good job was what I was supposed to do, and I loved it. I never saw myself as a prisoner of my situation. But the truth was my husband and I were tied down. We budgeted tightly, often cutting it close at the end of the month, charging the credit card for groceries and diapers, and holding off until the next paycheck. And an emergency fund? We didn't have such a thing.

I was a prisoner of my own mindset. I never saw the ability to create more for myself. I thought "getting by" was just the way it was supposed to be. Disclaimer:

there is *nothing wrong* with loving the career you are in and wanting to stay in that career. But for me, once the potential of creating more was introduced to me through direct sales, I became curious about how to actually break free.

Throwing that book on my principal's desk, stating that personal development wasn't in the contract, reminds me so much of the prisoners in that cave. It reminds me how limited their scope of belief was—their understanding of the world outside of the cave. It reminds me that the bravest thing we can do is escape the thoughts we've adopted over the years and move away from our own shadows.

So let me ask you:

- Do you find yourself staring at the limited shadows in front of you, or do you find yourself starting to move into the light outside of your own cave?
- Do you wrestle with the things you've always believed are musts, like getting a good job and working until you retire?
- Do you want more for your life than what you currently have but don't know how to do it?
- Do you sometimes feel alone, shouting to others to see the potential they too have in front of them?
- Do you find yourself wondering if you're really cut out for success? If you're capable of building a direct sales business?

Friend, I am here to tell you that I was once that woman, struggling through the answers to the questions above, bound to the belief that living paycheck to paycheck was just life. As the woman who actually threw self-help back at a helping hand, as the woman who once stared at the shadows in front of her instead of seeing the possibility that lay outside of her, I am here to assure you that you, too, can break free.

I was so tied up in my own limiting beliefs that I didn't bother to look up. You have a choice to stay in the cave or turn around and begin running toward something greater. So what do you choose?

How Do You Break Free From the Chains?

(If you are singing Wilson Phillips' "Hold On" right now, you really are my people!)

One of the first steps toward building a direct sales business is acknowledging the truth of where you currently are. Maybe you picked up this book as your starting point. For others, maybe you're ten years into the business and looking for a fresh start. Perhaps you are a leader who needs a fresh perspective on how to educate your team on best practices. No matter how seasoned you are in the business, breaking free and embracing a fresh perspective on direct selling should excite you. There are likely two components of the business you're already aware of:

Direct sales **isn't** easy.

But direct sales **is** simple.

No, that's not a typo. The action you take in business is simple. Cultivating the mindset to carry forward with those actions, well, that's where it gets a little tricky. But don't worry, I've got you!

Breaking free from those chains isn't just about building your confidence, reading personal development books, or participating in every training offered by your company. It's acknowledging what you actually can control and letting go of what you cannot.

Early on in my business, when rejections were high and morale was low, a mentor offered a bit of advice to control the controllable. When we break it down, there really are only three things in business that you can control:

- Your actions
- Your reactions
- Your mindset

That's it. Nothing else. So, for me, controlling the controllable meant I couldn't throw myself a pity party when things didn't go as planned. I couldn't wish things into being easier. I couldn't stew on the person who swore that she was going to place her order before the end of the month and then never placed the order. My areas of control had to be my attitude, my choices, my goals, my vision, my desires, and my discipline.

The first step in controlling your controllables is acknowledging the truth of where you are, in this moment, and what actually got you there:

- Your actions
- Your reactions
- Your mindset

These are your controllables. In the coming chapters, we will break each specific controllable into real-life examples and practical takeaways, but let's also take a minute to consider what each controllable looks like.

Your Actions:

Let's not sugarcoat it. Direct selling isn't hard work, but it is heart-work. It requires discipline, consistency, a willingness to develop personally, and a thick skin. There are certainly no shortcuts, no secret formulas, and no fast tracks to results. Jim Rohn once said, "You shouldn't wish things were easier; you should wish you were better." But I'd like to take that one step further and propose we stop wishing altogether and start becoming. To get better at sales, you have to go out and invite. To get better at recruitment, you have to talk about the business. To get better at closing your sales, you have to have conversations. And none of these things happen accidentally. You can't build something by sitting and doing nothing. The truth is, there is no easy button to direct sales. You have to go out there and do the work.

Your Reactions:

You cannot always control the outcome, but you certainly can control the output. In 2016, during a personal turning point in my business, I felt like the tactics I had used to sell my products and talk about my opportunity were falling on deaf ears. I was tired of posting on social media without getting results. In other words, I felt like I was doing the work and not seeing the return on my time investment. I remember a conversation with my mentor who said to me, "Katy, you can be bitter, or you can be better." I wanted to get better. I wanted my business to thrive, and the choice to make it thrive was completely up to me. So I went to work. I researched selling strategies, attended live events, improved my customer service, and spent time training my team on what I was learning through the process. I made a decision to not get angry about the current status of my business but to become curious and learn how to become better.

As the owner of a direct sales business, I want to let you know that you will receive rejections. You will likely experience negative feedback about the business model. You will be ghosted. You will have customers who decide the product or the service isn't for them. You will miss the goal. You will experience setbacks. You cannot reach the highs of the business without experiencing the lows. *But what you do in the lows develops your character, your grit, and your belief. When reacting to situations, I've found time and time again that the best question to ask myself is, "Is this happening to me? Or is this happening for me?"* That one word, "for," can be the difference between failure and success. That one word can be the difference between pressing on or signing off. That one word is what will, no doubt, make or break your business. How you react to situations that don't go your way makes all the difference.

> *"The impediment to action advances action. What stands in the way becomes the way."*
>
> - MARCUS AURELIUS, *MEDITATIONS*

The obstacles you come up against are not necessarily negative or harmful, but can actually serve as opportunities for growth and progress. Think of your obstacles from a different perspective, choosing to control your reactions as the way to move forward. By controlling our reactions and viewing obstacles as a means to grow, we transform them into opportunities for success.

Your Mindset

Actions and reactions are completely in our control, but think of mindset as the lever that controls those two functions. The way you think about thinking determines the action and reactions you are presenting. Walter D. Wintle's poem, *Thinking*, sums it up perfectly.

"If you think you are beaten, you are
If you think you dare not, you don't,
If you like to win, but you think you can't
It is almost certain you won't.

If you think you'll lose, you're lost
For out of the world we find,
Success begins with a fellow's will
It's all in the state of mind.

If you think you are outclassed, you are
You've got to think high to rise,
You've got to be sure of yourself before
You can ever win a prize.

Life's battles don't always go
To the stronger or faster man,
But soon or late the man who wins

Is the man WHO THINKS HE CAN!

- WALTER D WINTLE, *THINKING*

Success in direct sales is a decision. Plain and simple. It's a decision to see it through, to work toward your vision with relentless, unquestionable (and maybe a little crazy) pursuit. When you fill your mind with fear, doubt, and disbelief, your thoughts become your reality. If you feed yourself a lie long enough, eventually it becomes your version of the truth. So, think of the lies that live in your mind right now, rent-free. The lie of:

"I can't!"

"I've been trying too long!"

"It's too hard!"

"I don't have time."

"Maybe I am not cut out for this."

Are those lies getting louder? The energy you put into your thoughts matters as much as, if not more than, the energy you put towards action. What you feed your mind, the story you are telling yourself, has a direct impact on the outcome of your efforts. So, let's explore!

What Stories Do Your Current Thought Patterns Tell?

Not too long ago I came across a video of a cancer survivor describing a vivid dream she had. It caught my eye because she was closing her eyes as she told the story, almost as if reliving the dream in real-time.

She described sitting high on a ski lift with a close friend, taking in the sights and breathing in the cold on the mountain top. But when she looked over, she realized her friend was slowly falling, sinking out of the ski lift, threatened by the vastness of space between the lift and the snowfield below.

She reached over to her friend, grabbing her ankle and holding onto her for dear life, panicking over the chasm of *what if?* Gripping her friend with everything she had, she described with vivid clarity the sudden relief that it would be okay. Not because her friend was safe, but because she had made a decision that, no matter what, she wouldn't let go.

She described the wave and power of peace that overcame her, knowing the struggle wasn't over but the decision to hang on no matter what was in her control.

When I heard her words, as a cancer survivor myself, I connected with every breath of her story, every high and low, every moment of panic and worry, and every moment of overwhelming belief that comes from faith in knowing that it would all work out for the good.

Why share that story? Why share a dream with no seeming connection? Here's why: because the belief a cancer survivor had in knowing that it would all be okay is the same belief we need to have as business owners. Belief in three key areas is absolutely non-negotiable:

- Belief in Ourselves
- Belief in Our Products
- Belief in Our Opportunity

Belief cannot be built from nothing. It needs a solid foundation from which to rise. Belief stacks itself up over time with consistency, experience, failures, and wins. You should probably know that you are likely going to have to work over time on building belief. In fact, it's probably going to be the easiest thing to do, but it's also going to be the easiest thing not to do. The educator who threw a personal development book on her principal's desk wasn't capable of building a multi-million dollar business; she had to grow her belief in the opportunity, in her products, and in herself over time. You will, too.

Remember, the type of person you are becoming matters far more than the goals you are achieving.

Let's take inventory of the current stories we are telling ourselves:

- (Action) What action are you consistently taking in your business? What action are you avoiding? Why? What is the gap?
- (Reaction) In times of stress, how do you react? Do you feel empowered when things don't work in your favor? Or do you feel let down? How might this be impacting your current results in the business?
- (Mindset) In what areas of your life do you need to break out of your own chains? What limiting beliefs are holding you back in the business?

On a scale of 1-10, with 1 being the lowest score and 10 being the highest, rate your belief in the following areas:

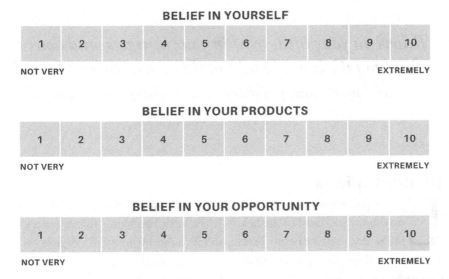

BELIEF IN YOURSELF

| 1 | 2 | 3 | 4 | 5 | 6 | 7 | 8 | 9 | 10 |

NOT VERY   EXTREMELY

BELIEF IN YOUR PRODUCTS

| 1 | 2 | 3 | 4 | 5 | 6 | 7 | 8 | 9 | 10 |

NOT VERY   EXTREMELY

BELIEF IN YOUR OPPORTUNITY

| 1 | 2 | 3 | 4 | 5 | 6 | 7 | 8 | 9 | 10 |

NOT VERY   EXTREMELY

Actions, reactions, and mindset are critical to success in the business. Remember, I've become a writer of self-help books—a far cry from the woman who refused to read them because it wasn't a part of the contract. We can't focus on where we want to go until we get real about any shadows that reside where we are.

Take a step back. You've already accomplished so much (and we haven't even gotten to the good part yet!) As we dip our toes into Chapter Two, we're going to break down The Belief Trifecta. As you look at your current scale, keep in mind that our goal is to identify the gaps we may have in belief that are preventing us from moving forward.

Go grab a cup of coffee and meet me back here tomorrow. Deal? (Or if you feel like charging ahead, great, I'll see you in the next chapter!)

Chapter Two

"Believe in your idea, trust in your instincts, and don't be afraid to fail. It might take multiple iterations, but with hard work and persistence, anything is possible."

- SARA BLAKELY

The Belief Trifecta

Let me paint a picture for you. Let's say you and the family decide to pack up the car and head to the beach. It's beautiful outside—there's not a cloud in the sky, there's a balmy breeze, and it's a mildly humid 85 degrees. When you arrive at the beach, you lug all of your coolers, chairs, buckets, and shovels to the perfect spot. Your toes nestle themselves into the sand, and when you look at the water, you do one of these three things:

1. You *run* full steam ahead, straight into that water, belly flopping into the waves.
2. You slowly put down and organize all of your gear, then gracefully walk to the water to dip your toes in.
3. You enjoy the view and the water from a distance, because that water is cold and wet sand is just too much.

Which one are you? If I had to guess, you might not be a belly flopper, but since it's hot, you slowly walk down to the water, keeping your toes cool and your shoulders warm. You may slowly ease yourself into the water, but there's no need to cannonball yourself into the water, right? Afterall, you are a *dignified* and *respectable* woman.

I've found most people in direct sales don't cannonball themselves into the business. Instead, they curiously dip their toes into the opportunity, not wanting to go all in too fast, a little hesitant that the opportunity might not be just right. But here's the thing: Belief grows the more we submerge ourselves into the waters of the opportunity.

Yours truly was a direct sales toe-dipper. When I first started in direct sales, I experienced the products. I used the products on my own and was getting results, so I became curious when I saw the woman (who later became my upline) talk about the business opportunity.

I got curious about how she was using the products to create income. I became curious about what her job entailed. I became curious about her lifestyle. And eventually, I became curious if it was an opportunity that might be open to me as well. In other words, I baby-stepped my way into the waters.

So how does one build belief? Chase curiosity.

As I mentioned, when I first started in direct sales I was a middle school teacher, but I was also coaching cross country, advising the middle school student council, and picking up extra duties like overseeing detention and the cafeteria to bring in extra income. On one occasion, I went to the grocery store to get a few essentials. It was right before payday. I knew that I had just enough to purchase milk and diapers for my son without having to charge the credit card.

The cashier, a sweet older man named Frank, who always went out of his way to say hello to me and talk to my 2-year-old son, rang up my diapers and milk that day. I handed over my debit card to Frank, knowing it was close to overdraft, but giving him no visible indication that I was sweating, hoping there was enough in the account.

He said the words that changed my life forever. The sweet cashier in the grocery store with a friendly smile and kind eyes looked at me and said, "Sorry, honey. It says insufficient funds."

Tears welled in my eyes as I frantically searched for the credit card, knowing that this was yet another charge that pushed us further and further away from the debt-free dream.

When I walked back to the car with the 2% milk, the off-brand diapers, and my teething 2-year-old son, I remember clearly thinking, "There has to be more to life than just getting by."

I had the realization that just getting by wasn't enough. The realization that I never wanted to hear "insufficient funds" again. The realization that having a great job wasn't getting our family to where we wanted to be financially. It sparked the question, "How does anyone do more than just get by?" I was curious, desperately curious, toe-dipping-in-the-water-curious: "How does anyone do more than just get by?"

The answer, of course, was right in front of me. The answer was a direct sales opportunity. The answer was believing that a life of more than just getting by was something I was capable of. The answer was believing that products could impact others and the business opportunity was possible for women like me—women with no marketing, sales, or business experience. I was curious and willing to dip my toes in before taking a big, cannonball leap into the waters. What I'm saying is, small action builds confidence, which builds belief.

So, let's get our toes wet, shall we?

Build Belief in Yourself

There's this scene in my husband's favorite movie, *Dodgeball*, where the coach, Patches O'Houlihan of the infamous Average Joes (the dodgeball team), reminds his players that if you can dodge a wrench, you can dodge a ball. He then begins to throw wrenches at the players and they hustle and move and guard themselves from the flying objects. If you aren't a lover of slapstick comedy, I realize that this analogy is going to hit hard. (It was a pun, a possible failure of a joke, but stick with me, I have a point).

If you can share the products, you can share the business. If you can dodge a wrench, you can dodge a ball. The biggest obstacle when it comes to building a business, growing an organization, and seeing income growth comes down to you and the space that lives between your ears. I know. I know. You're probably a ninja at dodging the truth, but here's what you can't dodge any more. There is an internal wrench, a story, that you keep dodging instead of embracing the truth.

Your wrench may include but isn't limited to (in no particular order):
- The fear of what people will think
- The fear of failing
- The fear of failing… again
- The fear of succeeding
- The fear of looking stupid
- The fear of hearing "no"
- The fear of letting people down
- The fear of disappointing others
- The fear that you don't have what it takes
- The fear that you will spend money you don't have
- The fear of running out of people to talk to
- The fear of putting too much pressure on yourself

- The fear that maybe your mom (or aunt, friend, spouse, Susie down the street, whomever) was right about "this type of business"
- The fear of investing in yourself
- The fear that the market is too saturated
- The fear of not doing enough, not being enough, or not mattering enough
- The fear of_____

You can fill in the blank with about 100 other possibilities, or...

You can write a list of what could happen if it all worked out better than expected:

- The possibility of success
- The possibility of growth
- The possibility of freedom
- The possibility of living a life beyond your wildest dreams
- The possibility of proving others wrong
- The possibility of proving yourself wrong
- The possibility of creating new friendships
- The possibility of retiring early
- The possibility of leaving your day job
- The possibility of never worrying about the groceries again (a personal favorite)
- The possibility of making an impact beyond the income
- The possibility of being the fire starter who creates an explosion
- The possibility of living in a way you once never thought possible

I don't know about you, but I'd rather paint the picture of possibility than throw the wrench of fear. I would rather cast the vision of what can happen when I don't let fear write the story. So, what's your picture of possibility? Write it out below!

_____

_____

_____

_____

Build Belief In the Products

Over the years, I've mentored hundreds of women in my own direct sales business as well as through the services I offer through Chic Influencer. Often, when women start a business through direct sales, they see the glamor of what others have achieved. They want to know exactly what to do (and don't worry, we cover that in Section Two). But before I ever jump into action, I ask clients why they're building a direct sales business and why they chose the business they did.

It's not enough to just build a direct sales business, you have to:

- Believe in the products you offer
- Use the products you offer

I am often shocked to hear direct sellers who want to build a business but have no interest in using the products they endorse. It's kind of like when I was buying my Jeep® (side note: I *love* my Jeep! Jeep-wave to all my fellow Jeep drivers). At the first dealership we went to, Jeeps were on the lot, but the salesman did a terrible job trying to sell us a Jeep. He was trying to sell us a car. He couldn't tell me about any of the features. He didn't provide any testimonials of clients who had joined the Jeep Club. And he didn't seem excited about what driving a Jeep would look like for me.

I am not a car salesman, but I love my Jeep. I would highly recommend driving a Jeep. And I love seeing other Jeep drivers on the road when the top is off, because we just get it. It's obvious to those who know me: If I was going to go into car sales, I would be selling Jeeps.

Jeep driver or not, we all know what it's like to be sold to. We all know what it's like to see friends online sharing their businesses who actually have no passion for what they do. And maybe we're all just trying to make a buck, but I can say with certainty that the second car salesman (Jack was his name) was likely seeing *far* more sales and commissions because of his own belief. Car Salesman One (I don't recall his name) offered us a product called a Jeep. My man, Jack, sold us the experience of living the Jeep life.

Jack helped me select the right Jeep for me and walked me through his own experience with his '05 Wrangler. He talked about different features, considerations, and all the bells and whistles. He was honest about what he didn't think I needed, and what he thought (after getting to know me) I wouldn't be able to live without. Yes, those running boards were a good idea for all five feet of me.

Here's the deal. The first car salesman was just trying to sell another car, move that inventory, and cash that check. The second car salesman sold me on the experience of owning a Jeep. He was creating a picture of what it would be like to own a Jeep—off-road, top-down, summer nights… you get it. Let me be clear;

both men were trying to sell me a Jeep. However, one man was selling me a vehicle and the other was selling me an experience.

In direct sales, you can't just sell someone your product. If you want to stand out from the crowd, you'll need to sell the experience, and in order to sell an experience, you have to actually *experience* it for yourself. If I had a mic right now, you know I'd be dropping it, right?! Believing that someone else would be better off because of the products you share with them changes the experience you give them. When you believe in your products, you don't sell the products, you sell the experience.

How to Sell An Experience

1. *Use the products.* If you are part of a direct sales business that totes a catalog of products, you do not need to share them all. Instead, I encourage you to select 1-3 products that you love and want to talk about regularly. The goal is to showcase what problem(s) these products can help your ideal customer resolve or what desire your products help your customer fulfill. You are guiding them to a solution, but it's hard to speak about the impact the products have if you don't have experience, right?

2. *Paint a picture of how the product can positively impact someone else.* I'll cover this in more detail in the coming chapters, but think about my experience purchasing Betty (yes, my Jeep absolutely has a name, and yes, of course, it's Betty). The first car salesman talked about the features, the bells and whistles, but it was *obvious* the man just wanted to collect his check. The second salesman had first-hand experience and walked me through the experience of owning a Jeep. He even went so far as to tell me some of the top trails I would need to test out. Both men had the same goal, but their approach was different. One tried to sell me a product. One sold me on the experience. What is your current approach?

3. *Keep honesty as your policy.* Okay, I know what I am going to say might be controversial, but when you sell an experience, you are selling in the best interest of the customer. And what's best for the customer isn't always going to result in a sale or a sale of the product with the highest commission. An honest approach to your products goes a long way. I remember when I started in direct sales, our company reformulated one of its most popular products. Guys, I hated it with a passion. It was terrible. I get queasy thinking about the chalky, metallic taste of what was once my favorite product. As scary as it

was, I reached out to my very small customer base and let them know what to expect from the formula. At the time, with only a handful of customers, I experienced a lot of appreciation. As the product was reformulated again, my customer base went up and more customers were brought to me from referrals! It was a win for all. But take it from me, honest sales feel good, and those customers, more often than not, keep coming back.

Build Belief in the Opportunity

"Your success in direct sales is determined by your actions. Your actions are determined by your habits. Your habits are controlled by your thoughts."

- MELANIE MITRO, CHIC INFLUENCER

Can I be completely transparent? I apologize for what I am about to say, and mean no offense to anyone, but if I wasn't going to be *completely* honest with you, not only would there be no point in writing this book, I think you'd miss one of the most important steps in building a direct sales business. In most cases there are two ways to build a direct sales business:
- Selling the products
- Leading an organization of distributors

My upline was successfully building both when I started my business. Our lives were very different a few years ago. She was a full-time mom with more flexibility to build the business. I was a full-time teacher working overtime and trying to make ends meet. While starting the business, I was plugged into weekly trainings led by leaders in our large organization. On one particular call, I was elbow-deep in a sink of dirty dishes, listening to the leader talk about the life she had built with the opportunity. Full disclosure: this woman was next-level gorgeous—a young, beautiful, successful blonde who spoke with confidence and conviction as she shared the story of visualizing her dream wedding on the Amalfi Coast at sunset. The picture she painted drew me in; I found myself shaking my head, "YES! I want that!" I was motivated, inspired, and ready to set the world on fire, until…

… until I returned to a sink filled with dirty dishes, a load of laundry that refused to fold itself, and a stack of papers that I promised my students I'd have back to them the next morning.

Truth be told, after I left the vision of what she was living and returned to the reality of responsibility, her motivation became "good for her," but it wasn't enough to be a "maybe I can, too."

Letting you in on a little secret: Your vision doesn't have to be big at first. I feel like every time I say this I get kickback from top industry leaders who have that big vision mindset. But the truth is, most people aren't wired that way, including yours truly.

What I needed to succeed was to build my belief through smaller experiences. So, instead of focusing on the big wins, like a wedding on the Amalfi Coast, I had to create a vision filled with small wins.

I asked myself, "Katy, wouldn't it be cool if … ?"

My first big vision for my business was to get the groceries paid for. I asked myself, "Wouldn't it be cool if I could get the groceries paid for?" That's it. It was an additional $150 a week. The thought of being able to do that blew my mind, but it also felt doable and within reach. Then, as I began to achieve small goals like getting the groceries paid for, I found the courage to create a bigger vision: adding a car payment, taking a vacation with my family, eliminating debt, purchasing our dream home, and paying for private school for our boys.

When I started in direct sales, it became easy to get star-struck by the potential and grab onto the visions that others cast instead of owning my own vision.

To this day, I keep saying to myself, "Wouldn't it be cool if … ?"

I had to grow into the woman who believed she was capable of making her own vision of success her reality. By defining success for myself, and allowing myself to visualize a "wouldn't it be cool if" life, I started to truly live it.

What about you? What is your crazy "wouldn't it be cool if" statement? Remember, it doesn't have to be grand. It just has to move you into action.

Whether you are a big vision thinker or a small action taker, create a picture of your crazy-cool life. What do you believe you can do through the opportunity you've been presented with? What would your life look like if you went and did the dang thing? Dream big on your own terms. Make no apologies for how big or small that vision is! It's yours. Now, get to work.

Share Your Vision

Melanie designed a recruitment course to help women share the business opportunity in a way that helps them build their team. In the direct sales model, recruitment is defined as onboarding new distributors to build the business alongside you. In most cases, you receive commissions based on the performance of your organization as well as your own sales. In order to sell the opportunity, you have to believe in the opportunity. When you believe in the opportunity, your vision begins to take life and you begin to jump into action. And guess what? You aren't the only one jumping into action! Belief in your opportunity gives permission and confidence to others to begin stepping into action. Believing that your company is the vehicle to help others drive toward success is essential to building a business.

 Scan the QR code to learn more about The Direct Sales Done Right Recruitment Course!

Consider the following:

- Do you have the belief that you have the ability to figure it out along the way?
- Do you believe that your company is the vehicle to help you drive toward your goals?
- Do you understand your company's compensation structure?
- Do you understand the multiple ways you can generate income?
- Do you believe that others can see success through the business opportunity?
- Do you believe you have the tools (or access to the tools) to guide others in the business?
- Do you have the desire to support people through your business opportunity?
- Does the thought of leading a team excite you into taking action?
- Do you share your vision to paint a picture of possibility for others?

Vision Casting Done Right

I've heard countless speakers talk about vision and manifestation. Most of them share the concept the same way: Dream big and take massive action! While I can appreciate their excitement about the big vision, I think they often leave out a critical step. Here's the deal: Vision boards are pretty. I mean, who doesn't want to create a seven-figure business, or develop six-pack abs, or build a dream home with a dream car in the garage and a white picket fence in the front yard? Yes, please! Count me in for one of those.

I get it. You have to picture what you want, draw a line in the sand, and—BOOM—take massive action. Visualize it, build it, and, straight up *Field of Dreams*-style, it will come.

Until it doesn't come.

Until that vision board you took such care to create ends up buried under a pile of unread personal development books. Until that picture you wanted gets blurred out by rejection, by "I can't," and by the reality of daily responsibility. Until that vision board gets put away for another day, another month, another year, another life.

Sound familiar? Here's what can make the difference between the vision of what you want and the reality of what you are working toward: You cannot sit idly by waiting for the vision to be manifested. **You have to care more about the action than the outcome.** You have to take really boring, mundane, and sometimes slow, seemingly insignificant action every day. Sure, your vision board matters if, and only if, you are taking the right action daily that will help you achieve it. And let's be real, that part isn't pretty. No one throws a "get gritty party" (but maybe I should. I don't know. I'd totally bring cake). No one wants to glorify the grit. I see it all the time: push goals, vision parties, and manifestation meetings. Meditate. Visualize. Pump your arms. Dream big. "IT WILL HAPPEN!"

It won't.

For visualization to work, you have to believe that you are capable of making that vision a reality. If it feels too out of reach, it will be out of reach. If your grand vision doesn't feel attainable, we need to shift our focus to mile markers along the way to achieving that grand vision. I couldn't bypass talking about mindset to kick off our time together, simply because if we don't have the right mindset, action falls by the wayside. If action falls by the wayside, so does our vision. So, how do we actually keep moving forward? How do we continue to work toward our goals when they seem out of reach? We cannot only talk about the big vision, the someday, the not quite within reach. We have to get into the habit of talking about the mile markers that are right in front of us. I call this concept "Driving Toward Daylight." Chapter Five provides a more extensive look into this concept, but it's imperative to mention that our vision will not happen without an action plan. In other words, we have to blur out the end destination and allow our eyes to focus on the smaller achievements (mile markers) that are attainable because they are right in front of us.

Driving Toward Daylight

Let's break down how to cast a vision we can actually achieve.

1. *Cast the big vision.* Make it clear and feel it with all of your senses so that the thought of not achieving it actually aches—straight up hurts. For example, when I visualized the home we bought five years ago, I didn't just picture the big windows or the hardwood floors. I pictured the muddy shoes and popsicles in the freezer. I pictured the sounds of a crackling fire and the scent of homemade pumpkin bread on a Saturday afternoon. The picture was so clear in my mind that the thought of something taking it away actually pained me.

2. *Blur out the big vision.* This is critical. Take your hand and blur out that big vision! I know, I know. Sounds strange, but blur that baby out. Our attention and focus doesn't need to be on the end result. It needs to be on the action. Yes, our vision is still there; we are driving toward this, our daylight. But our eyes need to be on the smaller vision right in front of us!

3. *Focus on your mile markers.* Align your vision to action. Remember, setting smaller, achievable goals keeps your eyes focused on the action that leads to the desired outcome. These are the action steps that need to be taken daily. These mile markers tell you how much you have left to go as you close the gap between where you are now and where you want to be. In Chapter Six, we have an entire section dedicated to your mile markers called the Income Producing Activity Tracker.

4. *Divorce yourself from the idea of perfect action.* Imperfect action is much better

than perfect inaction. Life happens! Detours and potholes are a certainty on this trip! If it doesn't go as planned, revisit your mile markers.

5. *Celebrate the small wins along the way!* As we set smaller goals and begin to see results, we gain confidence and continue moving forward to the next mile marker, and the next, and the next (you get the picture)!

A personal note about casting the BIG VISION: Although I found other people's big visions inspiring, I knew that I needed to create my own vision. As I've mentioned, the big vision I set to achieve through direct sales was paying for groceries. It meant no more fighting over enough in the account. It meant I didn't have to feel guilty about purchasing diapers before payday. It felt attainable to me and it excited me. As this vision became *consistently* achievable, I cast another vision of extending my maternity leave. Then I cast another and another.

My point is this: Never let anyone tell you that your vision isn't grand enough. If it excites you and motivates you, that's what counts. After all, it's your daylight that you are driving toward. Take some time to write out what your personal Driving Toward Daylight journey might look like on the next page.

MY PERSONAL DAYLIGHT (BIG VISION)

MY MILEMARKERS

1. _____
2. _____
3. _____
4. _____
5. _____
6. _____
7. _____
8. _____
9. _____
10. _____

DIRECT SALES DONE RIGHT

Act As If Statements

"Start acting like the person you want to be and soon you will be that person."

- UNKNOWN

Act As If Statement (def): A statement of truth about the person you are in the process of becoming. It encompasses your actions, your reactions, and your beliefs that align with the person you are becoming.

Possibility is an essential picture to paint, but I would rather paint a picture of my reality. So, this is where we often get the question, "But how? How do I take the picture of possibility and make it my reality?" Of course, action is part of the process. But before we dive into the specific action, can we take a step back and talk about the daily practice of becoming the person who can achieve the vision we've set for ourselves?

We need to ask ourselves, "Who do I need to become in order to live out the vision I've cast for myself?" Have you ever sat down and thought about your thoughts? Have you ever really reflected on your thought patterns or your narrative loop? Our thoughts dictate the action we are going to take, and our actions become our habits. Habits are either moving us in the direction of our goals or further away.

According to the Cleveland Clinic, the average person has 60,000 thoughts a day. Of those, 95 percent are repetitive. On average, 80 percent of the repeated thoughts are negative.[3] Why does this matter? Because our narrative becomes our reality. If you think:

- "Building a business is hard!" Then it is.
- "I'm not good at sales!" Then you won't be.
- "I don't have time to focus on social media." Then you won't.
- "The market is saturated!" Then it will be, for you.

But if you consistently begin to think:

- "Building a business is fun!" Then it is.

---

3 Haley Goldberg, "The One Question I Ask To Stop Negative Thoughts From Ruining My Day," *Fast Company*, July 28, 2017, https://www.fastcompany.com/40444942/the-one-question-i-ask-myself-to-stop-negative-thoughts-from-ruining-my-day

- "I am a rockstar at closing sales." You are!
- "I make time to focus on building my business on social media." You do.
- "There are so many people who need my products!" There are!

Those thoughts compound and create our reality. So, how do we break the cycle of the thoughts we don't want and adopt the thoughts we do? How do we shift our thinking?

We need to act like the person we believe would be capable of achieving those goals before we actually become that person.

Act As If In Action

My upline always shared this story about how she timidly (almost accidentally) created an act-as-if affirmation statement. Years ago, when she had this ruminating thought of becoming the top leader in our direct sales business, she decided to write the words, "I am the top distributor," in lipstick on the bathroom mirror. Freaking herself out with the words, she hurriedly erased them as if that statement never existed. That is, until she got out of the shower and the foggy mirror revealed the imprint of the act-as-if statement. "I am the top distributor."

She describes her accidental act-as-if incident as follows:

"Every time I stepped out of the shower and saw the words, 'I am the top distributor,' on the mirror, I started to get excited about the possibilities. I visualized walking across the stage at the company's conference with my family and leaders. The more I created clarity in the vision, the more excited I became about the action steps I needed to take. Each morning, I reviewed my time blocker to ensure that I had tasks that were going to move me closer to that top spot. At the end of the day, I double-checked that I actually did the tasks that were getting me closer to the top spot. I bookended my day with a reminder of what I was working towards and the vision of what it would feel like to achieve the goal. The more I saw myself in the goal, the more I stepped into the role of the top distributor in the company.

Even when my doubts screamed:

- I'm just a small-town mom from Mars, Pennsylvania. Can I really do this?
- Is achieving this goal going to take too much time away from my husband and kids?
- Do I have what it takes to lead a top team?

- I have no idea how I'm going to achieve this goal!

My actions drowned those doubts out. I started to think about what a top distributor does throughout the day. I brainstormed a list of actions a top distributor took in her business:

- A top distributor invites people every day to join their team.
- A top distributor isn't afraid to host business opportunity events each month.
- A top distributor confidently posts about the business opportunity and the type of person she wants to work with.
- A top distributor confidently onboards new team members every single week.
- A top distributor constantly invests in her mindset and leadership abilities.

Then at the end of the day, I would reflect on my action, asking myself, 'Did my actions align with those of a top distributor?' I disciplined myself to take these actions consistently, and what I found was that the more I stayed focused on action, the less the fear and doubts crept in. I saw myself becoming the top distributor in the company, began acting like the top distributor, and stayed consistent until the fogged-up mirror became the reality."

- Melanie Mitro, *4x Top Network Marketing Distributor*

It's important to note that she didn't *wish* her way to the top. One day, instead of dreading the remnant words on the mirror, she decided to embrace them, thinking about the action it would take to become the company's top distributor. She started to think about what the action looked like, what a daily routine would look like, how she would carry herself, and how she would show up.

So, who do *you* need to become in order to achieve the painted picture of possibility? What act-as-if statement is waiting to emerge from the fogged mirrors of your own self-doubt? And who is the woman you need to become in order to achieve that act-as-if statement? Who do you need to become to remove the negative narrative and step into the truth about who you are? What self-limiting beliefs are you leaving behind now?

Listen friend, in the next chapter we are going to talk about routines. That's all fine and dandy, but guess what? If you need to keep this chapter on repeat, let me repeat myself louder...

"Your success in direct sales is determined by your actions. Your actions are determined by your habits. Your habits are controlled by your thoughts."

And guess what… YOUR thoughts are 100% your choice! Write your own Act As If Statements below:

So What Do I Actually Need to Do To Be Successful in Direct Sales?

Most people are looking for a magical formula, a secret sauce, or a simple solution to direct sales. I am sorry to inform you that I do not have a workaround. There isn't a magic pill or direct sales hack, however, there is a proven action plan. In fact, the action plan I used when I started is the same action plan I used even when my team grew to thousands. Is direct sales easy? No. Simple? Absolutely.

In Chapter Six, we will cover the Income Producing Activities you need to take in order to grow your business in detail. For now, let's briefly cover the three actions needed to grow your business as a direct seller.

1. *Cultivating a Community*: intentional connection and conversation with your ideal customer or team members (usually before the sale or sign-up occurs).
2. *Conversation*: beginning the invitation process, asking questions, inviting directly to the opportunity, overcoming objections, and following up.
3. *Customer Service*: nurturing and supporting your current customers and team members.

There is one more category that isn't directly connected to Income Producing Activities but is still essential to your growth in direct sales: personal and business development. As you are reading this book, I applaud you for developing your business by learning how to sharpen your skill set, but I will caution you. Too often I have worked with direct sellers who try to build a business on the good intentions of personal and business development.

Please hear me. Reading a book, listening to an audio, or attending a conference will not build your business. It can *help* you build your business, but we can't sidestep past action. We must make sure that building a community, having conversations, and creating excellent customer service are our non-negotiables!

Just to get it out of the way, I think this is a great place to add another word of caution. I mentioned that direct sales is *simple* but it isn't easy. The reason it's not easy is because of the story we are telling ourselves. Awareness of the narrative matters, so I want to raise awareness of four almost undetectable "gremlins" that can make your business feel impossibly hard:

- The Entitlement Gremlin: This gremlin expected it to come easily, assumed it was easier for someone else, and believed he deserved to reap what he hasn't sown.
- The Impatient Gremlin: This one expects that he should be further along with no hard evidence to prove his case.
- The Lazy Gremlin: This gremlin often disguises himself as busy-ness. He's buried in lots of ideas and training and well-meaning intentions, but he doesn't always show up for income-producing action.
- The Party Gremlin: This one shows up ready for the rewards but isn't really invested in the work.

None of these little gremlins fall into the growth mindset category, but all of them can make themselves quite at home in the fixed mindset category. They're tricky little monsters, often stealing potential right out from under us. Be aware that the gremlins can creep up on anyone, including you (and me)!

Section One: Takeaways and Final Thoughts

Let me repeat: "Your success in direct sales is determined by your actions. Your actions are determined by your habits. Your habits are controlled by your thoughts."

I've heard Melanie share the story about the foggy mirror countless times, but recently something about that story hit differently. Melanie's first reaction was to erase the possibility from the mirror and her mind. And maybe that's where you are, too. Maybe you have this tiny thought that keeps coming up, a dream within you that you keep trying to erase. Friend, I want you to fight that urge to put it to the back of your mind. There is a reason it's there. Instead, sit with it. Get curious about it and ask yourself, "Wouldn't it be cool if ... ?"

Of course belief and action work in tandem, so in Section Four, The Healthy Pipeline, I am going to lay out a clear action plan for you. But for now, let's review a few key takeaways from this section!

Please note: depending upon your business model, these activities may look a little different or may be called something altogether different. No stress! Reach out to your upline or a company mentor for more specifics.

Key Takeaways:
- Control the controllable. Your actions, reactions, and mindset are the only components of your business that you have full control over!
- The belief trifecta = belief in yourself, belief in your products, and belief in your business. You will not find success in direct sales if you don't have all three.
- For visualization to work, you have to believe that you are capable of making that vision a reality. If it feels out of reach, it will be out of reach.
- Act As If Statements frame your mindset to act like the person who is capable of achieving the vision you've created.
- There are three categories of Income Producing Activities for every direct seller: cultivating a community, starting conversations, and customer service.
- Be aware of your business gremlins!

Final Thoughts:
Confidence is a muscle. I'll never forget the first time I heard those words, thinking to myself, "Cool, what's the workout plan?" More often than not, well-meaning experts would share great one-liners and quick tips, but I genuinely wanted to know, if confidence is like a muscle, how does one strategically build it? This chapter is your workout plan.

First, we have to understand that we can only control what is actually in our control. That means instead of white-knuckling our business, we have to trust the process. We must trust that, as we take action in our business, we will grow our confidence. It doesn't happen overnight but over time. We get better at our approach. We get better at writing content. We get better at having conversations. We have to be aware of our reactions, getting curious instead of angry when things

DIRECT SALES DONE RIGHT

don't go our way. Most of all our mindset, the way we think of ourselves and our business, controls much of the outcome.

I encourage you to visualize. Remember, the type of person you are becoming matters far more than the goals you are achieving. The process of becoming the woman who is capable of achieving that goal is the path to success. Confidence and action go hand in hand; they complement one another. Action builds confidence. Likewise, confidence grows as you take imperfect action.

So, just take the messy action! Let it be imperfect. Let yourself make mistakes, and then get back up and go at it again!

Section Two

Of Course It's Personal, It's Business: Owning Your Role in Success

"If you dwell on your strengths, your blessings, your goals, and all the people who love you, you will attract even more blessings, even more love, and even more accomplishments."

- TOMMY NEWBERRY, *40 DAYS TO A JOY-FILLED LIFE*

Eleven years ago, with no previous experience in the direct sales industry, I joined a growing fitness and nutrition network marketing company. I had *no idea* what I was getting into. I had *no idea* what I was doing. No marketing experience. No branding experience. No selling experience. No team leadership experience. None of it.

I had experience as a teacher with an expected yearly salary. So, the entire selling industry, to me, was a wild change. Coming into the business, I wasn't taught how to set boundaries. I just learned how to set goals and how to hustle in order to accomplish them. What I didn't know then that I wish I would've considered as I was building my business is this: There is life beyond paycheck to paycheck. There is an opportunity to build a business beyond your wildest dreams. Cliché? Yes. But it's true. I've seen it. I've experienced it.

But it *is* a business. There are benchmarks, quotas, goals, and growth. It doesn't build itself. And with those benchmarks, quotas, goals, and growth have to come some serious boundaries. I didn't always build it right. I didn't always prioritize the things that mattered most over the goals that mattered in the moment. I'm not really proud of that. But when you know better, you do better. When you do better, you teach better. I want you to love who you are becoming through the process of building this business.

So, to the woman in direct sales who is in the thick of building her business, this section is all about setting you up for success. Not just success in sales, but success in how you build your business. *After all, what good is a business that looks good from the outside but doesn't feel good on the inside?* In this section we are going to talk about setting goals that prioritize the most important aspects of life, define what short-term sacrifices really mean, and the essential action steps toward success.

I want you to enjoy the process of building a business, because the challenge you endure is changing you! Visualize the process of working joyfully and what that will feel like for you.

What we'll cover:
- Creating Routines
- Make a Decision: Business or Hobby?
- Setting Goals as a Direct Seller
- Your Income Producing Activities
- Let's Track!

I've also filled this section with a few visuals to help you along the way! This section is going to provide a joy-filled approach to building a business you love.

Chapter Four

"Treat your business like a business, it will pay you like a business. Treat your business like a hobby, it will pay you like a hobby."

- EVERY UPLINE AND MENTOR EVERYWHERE
(Okay, I am being somewhat dramatic, but if you know, you know)

Make a Decision: Business Or Hobby?

Build your business like a business … or don't. Either way, you can win! I am going to let you in on a secret. I am sorry to any upline or sponsor offended by this truth, but if you want your business to be a hobby that creates passive income, that's more than okay. There. I said it.

I don't know who needs to hear this, but you can actually create a successful direct sales hobby. In fact, I think there's a lot of pressure put on direct sellers to build a wildly successful, massive business without expressing the exact reality of what that actually takes.

But friend, the magic of direct sales (besides passive income) is that it is your business. So, that means that you call the shots. You decide what you want your business to look like in terms of goals, action, and potential income.

- Perhaps your definition of success is getting the groceries paid for.
- Perhaps your definition of success is paying for your child's hockey season.
- Perhaps your definition of success is taking your husband on an earned trip through the company.
- Perhaps your definition of success is leading an organization of others who are using the products and sharing them as well.
- Perhaps your definition of success is being able to leave your full-time job to stay home with your kids.

Ask yourself what you want your direct sales experience to do for you. Do you want a hobby that creates income? Do you want a business that provides income?

And how much time in this season of your life can you devote to your work?

HOBBYIST VS. BUSINESS OWNER

yes no

- [ ] [ ] Are you the face of the products you sell?
- [ ] [ ] Are you currently active in your company?
- [ ] [ ] Do you make it a priority to listen to your company's call? (Live/Recorded?)
- [ ] [ ] Do you listen & implement team trainings? (Live/Recorded?)
- [ ] [ ] Did you or will you attend your company's annual event?
- [ ] [ ] Can you verbalize your WHY?
- [ ] [ ] Are you showing up daily on social media?
- [ ] [ ] Are you posting with purpose and strategy?
- [ ] [ ] Do you consistently hit your company's benchmarks?
- [ ] [ ] Did you finish a personal development book last month?
- [ ] [ ] Do you successfully implement a tool, tip, or strategy from each training you attend?
- [ ] [ ] Are you actively engaged with everyone on your team?

Total yes: [ ]   *Total no:* [ ]

If the majority of your responses are "no," you may have more hobbyist tendencies. This isn't a bad thing, but it's important that you view your direct sales business as a hobby, and your efforts (especially financially) will reflect that in your income.

When I started in direct sales, I didn't see the potential of a massively successful business. I saw the opportunity to get the groceries paid for, and getting those groceries paid for was a success. I was working full-time and overcommitting to other activities. That choice prevented me from having the time to work on another business, but I did have the time to create a hobby. I was able to go all in with the time I had available.

Your "all-in", whether that's four hours a week or forty hours a week, is enough. Just make sure you're realistic about how much you can commit to and align your goals with the time you have to commit.

Honor Your Nos So You Can Stick To Your Yeses

Starting in direct sales was nothing short of messy. With no background in selling and no experience using social media, aside from posting albums upon albums of my son (hey! I was a new mom!) on my personal Facebook page, I certainly didn't know how to:

• Figure out my avatar
• Speak to my ideal customer
• Share, not sell

I definitely didn't know a thing about creating healthy boundaries. I cringe thinking of some of my early content.

When I say I was a mess, I was:

• Wildly obsessed with my business (think #girlboss on steroids)
• Hungry to learn everything; read every book, listen to every audio (podcasts weren't really a thing then), and purchase every course
• Numbers-driven, accolade-driven, wins-driven, goal-driven, and income-driven

You name the business drive, and I was buckled up behind the wheel, cruisin' down the interstate, ready to crash. And crash I did.

I will speak in uncomfortable, transparent detail about the crashes (yes, multiple head-bound direct sales mistakes) in the coming chapters, but to start off our conversation about what I have learned in the eleven years since starting a business, I'll say this:

There are things that matter, and then there are things that *MATTER*. Never sacrifice what matters most for what matters only for a moment.

Hindsight of course is twenty-twenty, and while I would definitely approach my business differently—setting harder boundaries, executing a business strategy that aligned with my *real* vision, and ultimately creating routines that honored my other priorities—I don't think I would be here, writing this book, without those mistakes and first-hand experiences.

Let me take you back to the early days of my direct sales business. Picture this:

- I was working full-time as a reading teacher.
- My son was in daycare.
- There were piles of dirty laundry and a house to clean on the weekends.
- I had a stack of papers to grade almost nightly.
- I had a neglected husband who was used to spending evenings with me on the couch watching CSI.

On top of that, I was a "yes girl."

I don't know why, for so many of us women, the word "no" just isn't naturally in our vocabulary. Am I right? I was the ultimate yes girl. Need a coach for cross country? Absolutely I can! Need a detention monitor? Sure! Why not? Student Council Sponsor? I AM YOUR GIRL. Three dozen cookies for the bake sale? I got you covered.

You name it, my answer was "Yes! I am on it!" (I see you right now, likely laughing, shaking your head, agreeing to all the "yeses" in your life).

So, my fellow can-do friends, can I let you in on a little secret? When we say "yes" to a commitment, we also say "no" to something else. It's worth asking, do your yeses honor the things that matter the most in your life, the goals you are working toward, and the values you hold most dear? If you answered no, here is my cautionary tale that may provide some perspective...

Around three months into my business when my warm market was all but dried up, I didn't have anyone else to invite, I felt like I didn't have any time to work on my business, and I was struggling to keep up with the sales trainings, the invites, the social media posting, and the follow-ups. Not to mention I had a toddler at home to take care of! Somehow, in all of this, I also still had to figure out what was for dinner.

I was breaking. I didn't have time. I couldn't do it all. Then, a breakthrough happened.

My upline, Melanie, called me after noticing my quiet retreat from our team's Facebook group. In tears, I told her that I didn't have time. I couldn't build a business, be a great teacher, a great mom, and still fold the laundry. On top of that, I had a responsibility to coach cross country every day after school, leaving me little time to spend with Nick.

I was trying, feebly, to be everything to everyone. My quiet (temporary) resignation from the business wasn't because I didn't believe in it, but because I was doing what I see all too often: *I was setting unrealistic expectations of success for myself while still keeping up with the demands of everyday life.*

Hear me, friend, because we are about to go into the dark side of unsettled ambition. I want you to know that you can set big goals for yourself, for your business, and for your life. But at some point, you are going to have to set hard boundaries or you risk losing yourself in the process of who you are becoming. This is one reason why so many people quit before they see the results. They believe the lie that they need more time instead of believing the truth: You can create results in the time that you have.

I am so grateful that my business mentor guided me through this struggle by providing a different perspective on success and time. The conversation we had in the middle of my quiet-quitting looked like this:

Her: "Katy, how much more time do you need to work your business?"

Me: "I need like two more hours in the day! But I don't have it."

Her: "Okay, what does your after school time look like?"

Me: "I coach cross country four days a week, plus the occasional meets."

Her: "Okay. How much time is that?"

Me: "When all is said and done, about two hours a day."

Her: "Hmmm… okay. Is cross country helping you get to your income goals?"

Me: "I think! It's $500 for the season. That helps us a lot."

Her: "What does that break down to hourly?"

Me: "…"

Her: "If you had that time to devote to your business, would you be able to make up the difference? If so, how many sales would that mean?"

Me: MIND. BLOWN.

Bottom line? Lesson learned. I was so busy being a yes girl that I was unintentionally saying "no" to the things that aligned with the goals I had set for myself. I was so fixated on the short-term financial gain of cross country that I didn't even notice the outcome of the long-term loss. In other words, my yeses were not honoring the priorities I set for myself and my business.

Time is money. Be aware of your yeses. Our habits become our regular and sometimes unknowing yeses.

Like…

- Brushing your teeth
- Taking the dog for a walk
- Cooking dinner before 7 pm
- Drinking a protein shake for breakfast

I thought that quietly quitting my direct sales business was the only option. I was so used to seeing the short-term gains of trading time for income that I didn't see just how much control I had over my success. I had to be willing to sacrifice some of my own beliefs about work and income for something better.

I wish that I could sit across from you over a cup of coffee and confirm that you can adopt this same mentality: Your income is not limited to your time. I had to go through the process of unlearning what I knew about making money and clocking in and clocking out to learn a better way (not a perfect way) of changing our family's financial situation.

As I began to unpack this new way of thinking, I recognized that my habits would become a huge part of the success story I was writing. I was going to have to become keenly aware of the habits that were working in my favor and the ones that were preventing me from success. Habits become part of who we are, so in order to establish habits that support our business goals, we need to first look at our current daily routines.

But first, a tip for my friends who struggle with the word "no"…

When you struggle with saying "no" because you don't want to hurt someone's feelings or you don't want to be seen as rude, I want to remind you that saying "no" is not actually a "no" to a person but to a request. The good news is that it's a skill that can be sharpened over time until it becomes natural. According to an article published by Psych Central, a "no" is one of the greatest forms of self-preservation. These questions posed by the article are great considerations before making any type of commitment:

- Will saying yes prevent me from focusing on something that's more important?
- Does this potential project, opportunity, or activity align with my values, beliefs, and goals?
- What are my core values, beliefs, and current goals?
- Will saying yes make me even more tired or burnt out?
- Will saying yes be good for my mental health? Or will it worsen my symptoms?
- In the past, when have I said yes and then ended up regretting it?
- When am I more likely to accept a request I'd rather decline? How can I

reduce these challenges?[4]

Creating Routines

"How we spend our days is, of course, how we spend our lives."

-ANNIE DILLARD

Working in the wellness industry through direct sales taught me a thing or two about routines. More specifically, it taught me about routines that change every January. My direct sales business products were fitness- and nutritional-related, so it was no secret that every November and December sales would slow, only to see massive results in January because consumers had been watching and were finally ready to make a change. While January was met with excitement, by March the excitement had worn off. The grind had set in. Year after year, it became evident that those who made a January routine continue to stick throughout the year had a few things in common, all of which I believe apply to our businesses too. When we are creating routines that support our business, let's consider the following:

- A routine that is enjoyable.
- A routine that is tied directly to who you want to become.
- A routine that supports the action steps needed to build a business.
- A routine that is simple, without bells and whistles, that becomes predictably doable after a couple of weeks of implementation.
- A routine that becomes a personal habit.

Routines, in a nutshell, are the key to sustainable results. Sustainable routines become our habits. Habits create success. So, to create routines that support our business, we first have to review the routines we currently have.

In the words of one of my favorite mentors, Craig Groeschel, "Successful people do consistently what other people do occasionally." We have to get clear about what we are currently doing occasionally so that we can make room for new routines to be done consistently.

---

4 Margarita Tartakovsky, MS, "How and When to Say No," *Psych Central*, June 14, 2021, https://psychcentral.com/lib/learning-to-say-no

Let's audit!

I'm pausing here for a quick second to clarify that there is a difference between a habit and a routine.

Definition of a routine: A conscious (thought about) behavior repeated frequently, otherwise it dies out.

(Think about it: How many people start a workout routine in January? But how many people really make it a routine?) Routines are intentionally practiced.

Definition of a habit: An unconscious, repeated behavior.

We first have to establish the routine to create the habit. Before we begin talking about new routines, it's important that we do a thorough audit of our time and our actions. Below are a series of questions to consider:

First, take a look at your weekly calendar.

- What are your weekly must-do's? Work? Commitments? Appointments? Priorities? Kids' schedules?
- What are your weekly joys? Date night? Time with the family? Happy hour after work? Girls' dinner?
- What are your most common yeses that take up the most time?

Now, take a look at your daily calendar.

- What are the repeated activities in your daily life? Are there activities you've committed to that are preventing you from working your business?
- What daily routines give you energy? What drains you?
- What frequently repeated behavior is moving you in the direction of your goals?
- What frequently repeated behavior is preventing you from moving in the direction of your goals?

What did you learn about yourself? The good, the bad, the less than gritty? I know you want to succeed in direct sales. So, first, we have to create routines that become habits, and guess what? The only way to create business-building habits is to repeat specific, income-generating routines over and over again.

When I realized that coaching cross country was not aligned with my business goals, I finished out the season and said "no" to the spring running club. Looking at my calendar, I was able to create more time for the Income Producing Activities in my business that actually aligned with my goals. I audited my daily routines. I noted that I had a few unconscious habits that weren't helping me. I didn't need to watch TV every night. I could spend an hour on my business in the evening after my son went to bed. I could wake up thirty minutes earlier to send out my follow-ups and invitations for the day (letting prospects know that I would return to their message that evening) so that the inbox would be primed for my response.

Likewise, I made shifts in my personal life that honored my relationship with Mike. Thursdays became our on-the-couch-watching-CSI date night, while Monday night he handled the bedtime routine with our son so I could work late. I worked on Saturday mornings for a few hours and spent Saturday afternoons without my phone. I became aware of my yeses and less hesitant about using the word "no." It wasn't perfect, but looking at the routines I established years ago, I know they have become my daily habits that honor the priorities in my life. The same can happen for you.

Forming a habit requires a strict routine. To create a routine, the behavior must be repeated over and over, and over, and over … and, you know … over again, until it's not even a thought; it's just who you are. (This kind of sounds like those Act As If statements, doesn't it?)

Step 1

Create your direct sales routine. First, let's look at your calendar. What commitments come first? When can you commit to your business? What time is off limits for your work? Do the routines you are creating in your day align with the goals you are setting for your business?

Step 2

Practice those routines over and over and over and over and over and over again (making tweaks along the way) until they become a habit.

*A note about time blocking: A huge part of The Direct Sales Done Right Academy educates our students on how to establish strong routines. You can also learn more about our *Direct Sales Done Right Planner* and *Chic Influencer Time Blocker* resources that will help you implement your routines and align them to your marketing goals!

 Scan the QR code to get your copy of *The Chic Influencer Time Blocker & The Direct Sales Done Right Planner!*

Since I am feeling feisty, I'm going to let you in on a little secret of success. Come in real close, because it's almost so simple that it's borderline unbelievable.

The secret to success is to be BORING. That's right, be boring. Be monotonous. Be mundane. Be very unimpressive. How? Become your habits.

Now, before you tell me about how Direct Sales Susie with 177K followers is successful in direct sales because her life is *wildly* entertaining, the furthest thing from boring—I'm going to let you in on a secret about our friend, Susie. She's not as wildly fascinating as you think. Sure, she might have pizzazz and confidence and an enviable closet. But I'd venture to guess that the average day-to-day actions of the woman you look up to, no matter how massive her following is or how far her influence extends, are *far* from exciting.

Direct Sales Susie, as it turns out, is probably just consistently following through on her routines, routines that became quite unfascinating habits.

At the risk of ruffling some feathers, I've always found it irksome when women in direct sales do a captivating, sometimes jaw-dropping job of sharing the glories of the business, but by contrast they (leaders in the industry) very seldom talk about the actual grind. But trust me, they grind.

In fact, that woman you follow, her habits (the routines she practiced over and over and over again) aren't what people find fascinating. Perhaps she doesn't seem boring to you, but her habits, what got her to the success she is experiencing, are most definitely, grindingly boring.

Do you want to know why most successful people only share the glory? Because the grind isn't at all exciting or Instaworthy. But there is no glory without the grind.

So, as your mentor who is committed to teaching *Direct Sales Done Right*, this is what you should be on the lookout for… at every opportunity, seek to learn from the habits of those who are doing what you seek to do. Show me a success story, and I assure you there's a story of habit that's far more telling.

There's a saying that I have used for years, "Success leaves clues." But I think there's more to it than that. Success is the story of the uncharming, relentless habits that create routines.

Success leaves clues, but habits will tell you the whole story.

Chapter Five

Setting Goals As A Direct Seller

Now that we've established realistic expectations for our business (or hobby), we can begin to create an action plan to achieve those goals! Whether you want to have additional income for date nights or you are looking to build a significant full-time income through the opportunity, belief and action are crucial to the outcome you are aiming for! In Section One we covered belief and mindset, but what good is believing without implementation? I refuse to let you stay stuck in thoughts of succeeding without giving you an actual roadmap to winning.

It's time to talk about goals. Now, before you roll your eyes and skip ahead to the secret to success, found in Section Six (just kidding, there's no secret! That's why I had to write a *whole* book), I think right now is a good time to tell you a story about *that one time*.

I was on an extended maternity leave after the birth of my second son, Dom. I set a goal to extend that maternity leave and worked hard to achieve it. Success achieved. The end.

Yeah, right. Here's what really happened …

I was on an extended maternity leave when I was diagnosed with Stage 4 cancer. I had forfeited my own health care benefits from my school district and was left without health insurance. I was thirty-one. My sons were three and three-months-old. I was a direct seller endorsing fitness and nutrition products, and all I could think was, "I am going to be sick. I am going to be bald. Who in the world would want me as a health coach?"

Guys, I was scared. Medically, I was scared. Financially, I was scared.

But the path I took toward business success over the following months as I battled cancer drastically changed how I ran my business moving forward, how I mentored my team, and how I created sustainable success as a direct seller. It also gave me a unique perspective on time and priority.

It was a crazy year. While I battled cancer and started to run a direct selling business in the wellness space, I grew my business by 300%, left my career as an educator, and became a full-time direct seller.

In Chapter Three, I introduced a concept known as "Driving Toward Daylight," but what I didn't share is how it became a lifestyle I adopted through my own personal Stage 4 cancer battle. The way I approached my cancer is the same way I learned how to approach my business.

Driving Toward Daylight

"Based on the progressive stage of your cancer, we are going to begin administering a heavy dose of chemotherapy. Our goal is to administer twelve rounds of treatment, continue scans and blood work, and make adjustments to the plan as we go." Words no one wants to hear.

There are two things that I didn't realize about cancer until I was personally in the thick of it (well actually about one hundred things). Two of the most obvious realizations were:

1. The comfort that comes from having a plan in place.
2. The frustration that comes when the plan in place isn't working.

As a business owner, freedom comes from knowing that the action you are taking will, without a doubt, lead to results. Except, of course, when the action doesn't lead to results.

Listen, friend. I get it. It's so frustrating to take action in your business and feel you are doing everything right but not getting results. It can be daunting to pivot over and over again to the point where you feel like you're just pivoting yourself into circles instead of getting results. But here's what cancer taught me about setting those goals and taking action: keep going. Keep Driving Toward Daylight.

"You have cancer and we anticipate it's going to take months of intense chemotherapy to eradicate the disease. Oh, and you are going to lose your hair, you're going to be sick, and you will likely have radiation to assure we've gotten all of it."

Whoa. Talk about one hard pill to swallow.

Truth be told, I couldn't think about the long-term side effects of the intense chemo treatments and what they would do to my body. I couldn't think about being sick. I could only think about the one step ahead of me.

This is Driving Toward Daylight.

Driving Toward Daylight, def.

An intense focus on the road directly in front of you instead of the destination you are working toward.

Picture this. You're heading down the highway with the roof off of your Jeep

73

(maybe the doors off too, depending on if the kids are in the car), the wind blowing in your hair, and you have about 400 miles until you reach your destination.

As you drive, you keep your hands on the steering wheel between the ten and two positions, and your eyes are fixed solely on the road ahead of you. You've blurred out the distraction of the world around you and well into the distance is your destination.

When battling cancer, I learned that the quickest way to spiral into worry, what-ifs, and overwhelm was to think about the battle still ahead. I had to mentally train myself to keep my focus on the daily battle right in front of me, undistracted by the worry of what-ifs as my hands remained on the ten and two and I drove on toward the destination: cancer-free.

Having a plan in place for your business is essential to know exactly how to achieve your goals, but what I find most direct sellers do is fall into the trap of what-if, or, "I keep trying and it isn't working," instead of focusing on the road right in front of them.

In a nutshell: Know your end destination and blur out that big vision. Put your hands on the ten and two of the steering wheel to avoid distraction. Focus on the mile markers right in front of you.

I persevered mentally, physically, and emotionally through my cancer journey one treatment, one recovery, one scan, one mile-marker at a time. In the same way that I focused on my battle with cancer, I focused on building my business.

I knew that I had to use my income through direct selling to help offset the cost of treatment. I started focusing only on the action I needed to take in any one given day, undistracted by what others in the business were doing and who was doing it better than I was. I focused only on the work that was in my control and paid attention to what was leading to results and when I needed to course correct.

When you are Driving Toward Daylight, you are undistracted by what's down the road because you only see the road in front of you.

Yes, you need a destination. Yes, you need to know how to get there with a plan. Yes, you need to take action. Yes, you need to let go of what isn't in your control. And yes, you need to trust the process.

With twelve rounds of intense chemotherapy and quite a few pivots and delayed treatments along the way, I entered remission about ten months after diagnosis. I'll repeat, the year I battled cancer and started Driving Toward Daylight, my business grew 300%. Without a doubt, Driving Toward Daylight will impact your business.

Now, before we move on, I think it's time to pause and think about how you are Driving Toward Daylight. Are you focused on those mile markers? Are your hands placed on the wheel at ten and two, with a road map in front of you? Do you have a clear vision of where you want to go, as well as the specific steps it's going to take to get there?

Truth be told, I didn't know how it would all turn out. But I did have an overwhelming feeling that it would all work out, that the drive I was on was leading me to a greater destination than I could even imagine. With tears in my eyes, I know that part of that journey led me right here, to the words on this page, the book in your hands, and the belief that you too can be infinitely blessed through the opportunity in front of you. Keep Driving Toward *Your* Daylight.

Accountability

I read a story this morning about a girl who went to the gym and the front desk receptionist looked at her with pity and said, "Wow. You've gone fifty-one days without coming to the gym. Do you realize that?" The woman took her card, smiled politely, and walked to the locker room with tears in her eyes.

She was embarrassed because she just couldn't find it in her to go. She tried. She had good intentions. But she just couldn't make it a priority. Fifty-one days. Had it really been that long?

While in the locker room, she confided in a sweet woman who said, "There's a spin class tomorrow morning. I'm going to save you a bike and I will workout with you." The next day, the woman didn't want to go. She tried to talk herself out of it. But she knew that bike was waiting. She knew that sweet woman was waiting. So, she walked in, pulled her shoulders back and said to the receptionist, "I'm back again. Day two."

I'm sharing this because, for people like the woman on day two, accountability is key. I'm also sharing it for the women who save us a bike. The accountability you create is key. When you realize someone is waiting for you to show up, it makes showing up matter more.

I get it: Sometimes we want to be left alone, unbothered, quietly chugging away at our work. But we need people to see us, we need people who challenge us. Proverbs 27:17 proclaims: "As iron sharpens iron, so one person sharpens another." You aren't meant to do life and work alone in order to make yourself better; there is a mutual benefit of making others better together.

Right now is a good time to ask yourself:
- Who in the business do I look up to and why?
- How can I add value to the goals they are working toward as much as they can add value to mine?
- Am I willing to learn from her and be challenged by her?
- Who do I believe will speak the truth, even if it's hard to hear?
- Who has similar goals to me but approaches them differently?

An accountability partner shouldn't be a mirror of you. It should be someone who thinks differently, acts differently, and approaches her business totally differently than you do. The first time I achieved elite status within my company, I partnered up with two other women in my organization. Both women were completely different than I was, unapologetically themselves, and adopted a fierce growth mindset. I won't lie, at first these women intimidated me, but I reached out and made a decision that we were going to achieve that elite status together, or not at all. I didn't realize that working alongside them didn't just keep me accountable, it helped me uncover some of the gifts I brought to the table.

While Deidra was fiercely outgoing and bubbly, Alyssa was confident and unafraid of any judgment. I, on the other hand, showed them how I marketed more strategically through my content and my conversations. For about twelve weeks we worked hard, pushing each other to new levels, picking each other up when we wanted to give up. We put aside our pride and challenged one another to reach higher. In other words, we were all iron, sharpening one another. Was it uncomfortable? Absolutely. Did it stretch us? You bet. Did we all achieve the goal? We sure did. Give others permission to hold you accountable and sharpen that iron, together.

Making Your Goals A Family Affair

Working in direct sales when your kids are little can sometimes feel like a juggling act. By the time my younger son, Dom, was toddling around the house and my older son was in kindergarten, I remember feeling pangs of guilt when I was working on my business. At the time, I was working my direct sales business full-time, but I was also attending live events and hosting many evening calls. My working hours were sporadic (thank goodness I started time blocking), and I was often hit with mom guilt for never feeling fully present with my kids because my thoughts were trailing into work. I want you to know this is a huge struggle for so many women in the industry, and many tools to combat some of those struggles are sprinkled throughout this book. But I want to share one strategy I implemented when the kids were old enough to understand work but too young to understand the necessary sacrifices.

My husband and I started to set goals that had nothing to do with titles and bonuses and everything to do with how our entire family would benefit. Let's be honest, your kids know you and love you as Mom, with or without your business wins. So, we started setting goals that benefited our kids, too, and used them to explain why Mom was working when they craved my presence.

On one occasion, we put a picture of a cruise boat up on the refrigerator, letting the kids know that Mom was working toward a trip for all of us. We talked with them about the fun things we'd get to do on the cruise and the sights we'd get to see. We painted a picture of possibility as well as hard work. In the evenings I would work and reference the picture.

This isn't a foolproof strategy, but it's something my young kids started to understand early—that I wasn't just working to work, I was working for us.

Added bonus: When you put a goal out there that your kids stand to gain from, whether it's a trip, a dance class, or a fun mommy-daughter day, connecting it back to the goal adds a layer of accountability. I know I certainly didn't want to have to explain to my kids that we weren't going to be able to go on that cruise!

What Does a Direct Seller Actually Do?

As you read the section about Driving Toward Daylight, it's likely that you were wondering about those mile markers I kept talking about. What are the mile markers, the activities that will lead you one step closer to success? It's easy for me to say, "Blur out the big vision and focus on the mile markers right in front of you." But what good is focusing on mile markers if you don't actually know what they are?

I will never forget listening to a leader in the industry share her secret to success. I had waited days for her training. I couldn't wait to hear her strategy for personally signing up over fifty distributors in one month! I was hungry to hear about her hustle. I brought a notebook to the call and took a shot of pre-workout (although it was 9 pm) to make sure I was *ready*!

The training began. She shared her story. She shared her success. She shared how she almost quit, but no, she didn't give up.

And I sat there, my notebook burning to be written in, waiting for the secret. As the hour went on, I became anxious by the time she was ready to answer questions (it could've been the pre-workout, who knows?) Without being prompted, I clicked unmute, cleared my throat, raised an eyebrow, and asked the question that the 100 other distributors on the call were likely wondering…

Me (tingling from the pre-workout): "Yes, but like, *how*? How did you sign all those distributors? How did you close that many sales? How did you sign them up?"

Her (confused): "What do you mean?"

Me: "What did you actually *do* to close all those sales? What did you actually *do* to bring on new distributors?"

Her: (Long pause)

Me (questioning the past hour I spent on the call, as well as my decision to drink a pre-workout at 9 pm): "…"

Her: "Gee. I don't know. I just kind of did it."

Me: Blank stare.

"I just kind of did it." What?!

What I know now, having mentored thousands of women in the industry, is that the people who are seeing results in their business have a sustainable strategy, simple action steps (that are repeated daily), and can list off exactly what they do. I promise, no, pinky swear, that I cannot and will not leave you hanging. The mile markers to success are simple. There is a direct connection between Income Producing Activities (which I'll cover in Chapter Six) and the results of direct selling. But it's not a do-it-one-time or do-it-once-a-week thing. The action I describe needs to be done daily, consistently, over days, weeks, months, and years.

So, maybe that is it? Maybe the real secret to success is hidden in Chapter Six (just imagine me winking here).

Your Income Producing Activities

Okay! Maybe, like me, you have the pre-workout jitters awaiting the secrets. You may even be tempted to turn ahead in the book looking for the action list to build your business. But before we go into the secrets, I need to explain why they matter. There are three key elements to building your direct sales business. Direct sales is a transaction of belief. The belief you have in the products you sell, the opportunity you share, and the experience you uniquely offer require you to build trust well before the customer or new distributor signs up. In order to see growth and continued revenue, we are going to talk about the action that creates a community, action that leads to conversion, and ongoing customer service.

The Three Key Elements to Making Meaningful Money

Community: Your community can consist of your in-person or social media following, friends, family, acquaintances, and colleagues. Your community isn't necessarily people who purchase from you (yet!), but they are people who would benefit from the products and services you offer. We want to make sure that we positively impact our community. Because much of our marketing is done through social media, many of the activities I share focus on cultivating an online community.

Conversion: We are going to brush fear aside and start taking daily steps to convert (lead people from interested to invested) people in our community into our customers or team members. Conversion is never accidental; it happens through consistently serving your community and inviting people to learn about your products and your business. You can create a community, but unless they know the doors are open to your business because you invite them, they will never purchase from you.

Customer Service: When customers are served well, they come back and they tell their friends. One of the biggest roadblocks for direct sellers is that they focus on first-time sales and forget about the people who've signed up! Serving people well leads to continued sales and potential team sign-ups.

Within these three elements, there is specific action we need to take to see continual business metrics. Since I am all for transparency, this is where you may be tempted to hold off on taking action until you absorb all the teachings, but waiting until you're ready or for the perfect time doesn't really work with me.

We are going to start taking action now.

As my partner at Chic Influencer, Melanie, always says, "Imperfect action is better than perfect action." Amen! So, let's let go of trying to be perfect. Instead, let's focus on taking a small step (driving toward that mile marker) and then another, and then another. You in?

One more word to the wise: Tracking. Do you currently track the action you take in your business? Conversations you have? Invitations you send? Follow ups that need to happen? It's such an easy thing to do, but it's a really easy thing to *not* do, too.

A few years ago, when I was looking to lose weight, I joined a program that helped me track my food intake using a point system. Now, we can debate about whether a weight loss program that forces you to track your food intake is sustainable, but what there can be no debate about is that tracking creates self-awareness. I became fully aware of my nightly need for my kids' Goldfish® crackers. I became fully aware that skipping my morning breakfast left me wanting to eat everything within sight by lunchtime. And awareness leaves room for improvement. You can't hide from your habits when they stare back at you, right?

When Melanie and I created the *Direct Sales Done Right Planner*, the weekly Income Producing Activity Tracker was an integral part of the product. The tracker allows us to see what areas of our business are thriving and what areas of our business need some improvement.

It's simple: Tracking reveals trends, trends reveal the truth, and the truth creates change. Within our direct sales business, being able to see on paper what action has been taken allows us to reflect on what works and what doesn't. So many women in direct sales track using their social media inbox or, worse yet, their memory, but they don't really write down the specifics of their actions. This only leads to feeling like they ran out of people to invite! Sound familiar?

When you know exactly what you're doing in your business daily, you can't hide from the truth of the tracker. Right in front of you is a detailed explanation of why you are or aren't getting results. Self-awareness as a business owner is a huge step toward achieving results!

Let's Track!
Your Action List for Building Your Business: The Secret to Direct Sales

Your community is your online and in-person storefront. Your mission in building a community is to bring awareness to who you are, how you serve, and what somebody stands to gain from working with you.

Action items to build and foster a community include:
- Being social, online and offline!
- Adding followers to your social media platform
- Connecting intentionally with social media followers and non-followers
- Creating social media content for brand awareness
- Creating social media content for engagement

Conversion starts with conversation. By building your community, you are intentionally creating content that brings awareness of your services to your audience.

When I work with clients one on one through The Chic Branding Experience, one of the first questions I ask about social media growth is, "Are you actively going out and seeking people to engage with, or are you waiting for people to find you?" The purpose of social media is to be social, so we can't hang around on our platforms waiting to be found!

The next step is to let people know that you are open for business *and* you want to work with them!

Action items to convert community (followers) into customers or team members include:
- Creating social media content for sales and opportunities
- Starting conversations with people who give you "eye contact" on your content
- Sending direct invitations to learn more about your product or your business
- Sending direct invitations for the business opportunity
- Following up with prospects

Next, providing exceptional customer service creates a noticeable impact on your business. In my direct sales experience, I quickly learned that while others spent a lot of time focusing on new sales, I could spend more time nurturing my current customers and offering exceptional service in order to gain repeat customers and build team members through a systematic approach to ongoing excellent customer service and support (more on this topic in Section Four).

Action items to create raving fans through exceptional customer service could include:
- Providing additional resources to help them on their product journey
- Creating a platform or group to engage with current customers
- Answering all messages, emails, and outstanding inquiries
- Serving as a liaison between your customer and customer service
- Asking for feedback and personal experience
- Sharing other products that complement the products they're currently using
- Inviting your loyal customers to learn about the opportunity

In Section Four, we will talk about The Healthy Pipeline and what it means to nurture your prospects and your customers in order to build loyalty.

Note: There are two other business activities that I left out of Income Producing Activities, on purpose—business development and personal development. While these two things are essential to building your business (hence why I am writing this book just for you!), your business will not grow without action. A member of our Direct Sales Done Right Community said it best, "Personal development without action is just reading for entertainment." Can I get an amen?!

I've found time and time again that many distributors put so much effort into developing their skills that they often forget to put those skills into practice. When I get asked, "How much time should I spend daily on personal or business development," my answer is always this: "When something you read or hear makes you want to take action, put the book down, or pause the audio, and go take action." *Development doesn't do much if we keep it tucked away on a shelf. Implementing what we're taught through action is the only way to yield results!*

Take a look at the Income Producing Activity Tracker taken from the *Direct Sales Done Right 52 Week Business and Marketing Planner.*

MY INCOME PRODUCING ACTIVITY TRACKER SAMPLE

Jan. 1, 2023

WEEK OF

		Mon	Tues	Weds	Thur	Fri	Sat	Sun
INCOME PRODUCING ACTIVITIES	**COMMUNITY**							
		Add Followers	12	20	10	2	15	5	0
		Intentional Connect with Followers *not an invite	5	8	3	5	7	2	0
		Social Media Post (Thumbprint Method)	1	1	1	1	1	1	1
		7-10 Stories	✓	✓	✓	✓	✓	✓	✓
		Highlight People: Testimonials/ Shout Outs	✓		✓		✓		
	CONVERSION	DM people who viewed, liked, commented, or followed	✓	✓	✓	✓	✓	✓	✓
		Direct invite to service, experience, or product	20	10	12	17	18	21	0
		Follow Ups	4	3	6	2	1	28	0
		Direct Invite to Business Opportunity	2	6	0	4	1	1	3
	CUSTOMER SERVICE	Ask for Referrals	1	1	3	0	4	1	0
		Engage with Current Clients	✓	✓	✓	✓	✓	✓	
		Answer Emails & Messages	✓	✓	✓	✓	✓	✓	
		Business Development	✓	✓	✓	✓	✓	✓	✓
		Personal Development	✓	✓	✓	✓		✓	

Section 2: Takeaways and Final Thoughts

Now that we have an action list of what it takes to build a direct sales business, it's time to move forward into our storefronts (our social media) and apply these practices. Remember, it's not about being perfect, it's about being consistent. Make sure your calendar gives you enough space to be taking imperfect action that honors the daylight you are driving toward.

Key Takeaways:
- When we say "yes" to a commitment, we are also saying "no" to something else.
- Success leaves clues, but habits will tell the whole story.
- Tracking reveals trends, trends reveal the truth, and the truth creates change.
- Your daily, boring action list is the secret to success.

Final Thoughts:
Be honest with me. When we talked about treating this journey as a business or a hobby, how did it make you feel? Did you feel a little relieved? Or did it go against everything you'd been taught? I get it, there's a fierce push for an all or nothing mindset. In the early days of direct sales, I was fortunate enough to be a part of an organization of highly driven individuals who were setting some mind-blowing goals, and in an awe-inspiring way, they were achieving them. I loved that I had an example of success right in front of me. I was learning from the best, but I also really loved my career as a teacher. At the time, I didn't want to pursue direct sales as anything more than a means of paying for the groceries. Over time, as my belief in myself and the business grew, so did my vision.

I encourage you to look at your own definition of success and honor that. A luxury of this business model is that you can define success on your own terms, and you should! That doesn't mean your vision can't grow. The business I set out to build when I started is vastly different from the business it became. I had to grow into the person who believed she was capable of achieving those goals. Look at your daily habits and your Income Producing Activities. Are they getting you closer to your own definition of success? Where is there room for growth? Whether you are looking for your business to help you to stock the fridge without breaking the bank or to create a full-time income for your family, it's your business! Success can only be defined by you.

 Scan the QR code to learn more about *The Direct Sales Done Right Planner* and track your daily activities!

Section Three

Serving Through Your Social Media: Your Winning Content Strategy

*"People don't care how much you know until they know
how much you care."*

-THEODORE ROOSEVELT

❝ We can absolutely make a strong assumption that an influencer with thousands of followers is going to be successful in business. It makes sense right? Have a lot of influence, you should have a lot of impact. Not so fast."[5]

- Jason Falls, *Winfluence: Reframing Influencer Marketing to Ignite Your Brand*

While researching specific examples for this book, I came across a case study of a very well known influencer. She has millions of followers on TikTok and a huge reach on Instagram. I mean, the girl puts up a post of a selfie with an emoji for a caption and still she attracts thousands of likes and comments. It's a safe assumption that this woman could sell anything and people would line up to throw their money at her, ready to purchase. Wanna hear something crazy? This influencer made the same assumption; certainly if they loved her, they'd purchase from her, right?

Wrong. No one. None of the millions of people who seemed to love her wanted to actually purchase from her. As the case study revealed, people are willing to give away a "like" for free, but their money goes to those who fill a different set of criteria. Followers purchase from you when they feel a confident "yes" in answer to two questions:

1. Do you care about me?
2. Can you actually help me?

There's a big difference between creating a brand that garners traction and leads to endorsements versus a brand that is developed to serve someone. A word of caution before we dive into this section: Likes on a post do not equate to sales. The amount of people following you will not be a direct correlation to your income. Instead, how you serve before the sale will give a more accurate measure of potential income.

So, take deep breaths and repeat after me, "Social media is my friend. Social media is easy. The algorithm loves me." Good! We agree! Remember those mindset practices from Section One? Let's reframe our thoughts with phrases like: "I love

---

5 Jason Falls, *Winfluence: Reframing Influencer Marketing to Ignite Your Brand*, ebook edition, (Entrepreneur Press, 2021).

social media," and, "Posting is effortless and I look forward to engaging with all my followers." If you've ever been the type of person to overthink social media or at least want to chuck your phone at the wall … If you've ever been the type of person to pour your heart and soul into a post only to have your mom "like" it and leave an unrelated comment like, "Don't forget to call Aunt Martha. It's her birthday,"… If you've ever been the type of person overwhelmed by all the well-meaning and overcomplicated advice of the industry experts…

You can now take a deep breath! We're going to uncomplicate the process and fall in love with social media. I realize I am putting high expectations on myself, but we can either spend time focusing on what isn't working, or we can get really curious about why it isn't working. Here's the truth: We can't be angry and curious at the same time. So, who's ready to get curious about social media with me?!

What We'll Cover:
- The Direct Sales Staple Story Strategy
- Why Most Direct Sellers Fail At Storytelling
- Passion, Knowledge, Profit
- I, Me, My
- The B.E.S Practices for Direct Sales Content Creation

Now, before we carry on, I want two things to be understood. First, this is a NO FAIL PLAN. Yes, I am making bold claims. But the truth is most people fail at implementing the plan. While we learn more about mastering the art of social media as a direct seller, we have to be real about our efforts. Consistency isn't an option, so you need to decide what that looks like for you, and then you've gotta stick with it. Think of your social media in terms of the law of inertia. You know, objects at rest tend to stay at rest, and objects in motion will remain in motion unless an outside force causes a change? *Consistently* show up on social media—on the platform, in the comments, and through your inbox. Here's why: The start and stop of social media will never move you forward. It will leave you feeling uncreative, like you are always doing something wrong, and like you're always a step behind.

Second, promise me that when you get frustrated, you take a quick pause and get curious instead of getting angry. Use your social media insights, talk to your audience, and evaluate your own content (don't worry, I will share how). But don't get mad about your content. Get curious. No matter how many people are following us on social media, our goal is to serve them well, so that when we do ask for a sale, they are ready to buy! Doesn't that sound amazing?! Let's get to work!

Chapter Seven

In 2011, a few months before I started my direct sales business, I had just put my son to bed and was settling in for an eventful evening of grading a large stack of my students' research papers. With a long night ahead of me, I did what any well-meaning procrastinator would do: I went to Facebook.

At the time, Facebook was relatively simple. Most people had a few friends who would share pictures of their kids or photo albums of events. But there was one girl who was posting what felt like all the time (insert eye roll). She was posting about health and fitness, and she'd talk about her meal planning and morning oatmeal (insert double-eye roll).

My initial feeling toward my fellow sorority sister was annoyance. There she was, talking about fitness and health, and (ugh) at the time I was really frustrated with my weight. But she was also talking about her business as a coach. I didn't really understand any of it. I knew she worked out, ate a lot of celery, and posted pictures of herself (my first taste of selfies), but I couldn't deny the fact that she looked, well ... happy!

So, back to me (supposed to be) grading those papers. There I was, a red pen tucked behind my ear instead of marking up the stack of papers awaiting their grades, scrolling Facebook; there she was, my sorority sister, face smiling out at me from a picture. She was with three other women in a car, all on their way to Philadelphia on a Thursday night. No husbands or kids, just a group of women in the car with their healthy snacks (again, rolling my eyes) on their way to a business meeting and a live workout. Then there was me, holding a red pen, waiting for the papers to grade themselves.

I immediately thought, "That's so weird. Who does that? Who just packs up the car for a weekend to galavant with a few girlfriends and workout? Also, who doesn't bring Combos® on a road trip? That's so weird."

My second thought when I saw the post was, "Must be nice. Must be nice to just hang out with your friends, take some time away, and make money working out."

My third thought was, "I could never do that."

And then, finally, I thought, "How do they actually do that?"

Here's what I need you to know about that story: She had planted a seed. She had evoked curiosity, not certainty. I didn't understand what she was doing or how she was doing it (and to this day it's a hard rule—you take the Combos on the road trip. I will never really understand her healthy-snacks-only rule of road trippin'). But I was curious.

For months, I continued to just watch her on social media, with her shakes, and her celery, and her galavanting. I never "liked" her posts. I never asked her for information. But the girl was consistent and energetic, and she just looked happy.

I bought a bootleg workout she promoted from Craigslist (am I aging myself here?) because I was too embarrassed to ask her about it. I didn't want her to know that she *gasp* had inspired me to take action.

But in a twist of fate, I ran into Melanie (the overly energetic sorority sister who'd managed to annoy and inspire me at the same time) at a restaurant and couldn't help but notice that she was radiating. I told her that I had been doing one of those workouts. She looked so happy, confident, and energetic. There was a spark to her that I quietly craved. That night, she messaged me on Facebook. I didn't even know that messages were a feature until I saw the notification! She simply said, "It was so great seeing you tonight! Hope you love the workout as much as I do! Let me know if I can send you a meal plan to help you get amazing results!!!!!" (Even her exclamation points were annoyingly happy.)

I didn't message her back. I just kept watching her posts (and I 100% realize this sounds stalkerish, but I am trying to drive home the point!)

In what likely seemed to her a random direct message from me, one day I inquired, "So, what is this business thing you do?" That message was actually the slow growth of the seed that was planted months before.

In the summer of 2012, I joined the direct sales opportunity with Melanie, the woman I had quietly watched and the woman who later became my business partner and co-author in *The Direct Sales Done Right Planner*. What started as a way to get the groceries paid for became a full-time career only a few years later.

I realize I've spent a lot of time sharing this story, but there is a deeper message in between the lines. For Melanie, she was simply taking action in her business, armed with the belief that consistency would pay off. She had no idea that on the other side of the screen, every day, was my growing curiosity for the business.

Now, I want you to look at this story from a new perspective. Take a look with a new set of eyes. What you've just read is a detailed example of a Staple Story. **The Staple Story is the repeated narrative you tell your audience about why you**

joined your business, or why you use your products in order to connect with them. It's a way for them to plant their feet in your shoes and connect to where you were before you started, the turning point that called you to take action, and ultimately where you are now because you made the decision.

In most cases, direct sellers should have two staple stories: a business Staple Story and a product Staple Story. Why? Because as direct sellers, we often market two services: the products and the business opportunity.

The business Staple Story showcases your business, how your life (and the lives of others) has been impacted by joining the opportunity, or how you came to see the value of the products you offer (likely a personal testimonial), but most importantly it calls your audience to action because they see themselves in the story you are sharing.

The product Staple Story showcases your personal experience using the product including any problems you experienced before using the product, skepticism you held, limited beliefs you had to walk through, and the results you've had or the experience you've had from using the product.

Breaking Down The Staple Story

There are three specific elements of a Staple Story. As a reading teacher, I often walked readers through what's called a plot diagram. In literature, a plot diagram is the hero's journey from the beginning to the end of the story. Of course, like all good stories, there are highs and lows and really great plot twists. But unlike a work of fiction, our job isn't just to connect to our audience and have them hear our story. We want them to gain the courage through our experience to begin their own adventure. Let's break it down.

1. *The "Before":* The "before" part of the story sets the stage. It illustrates the life you lived before the opportunity or the products impacted you. The purpose of the "before" is to connect to your audience and relate to what they might be struggling with, to show them that you, too, understand.
2. *The "Ah-Ha":* This is the climactic moment where a decision or realization is made that changes the trajectory of the story. Sometimes an "ah-ha" moment is clear, and sometimes it's a series of small events that lead to a change.
3. *The "Who You are Becoming":* I hesitate to call it an "after" because we are always evolving! But these are the ways your life has been positively impacted because of the business.

THE 3 ELEMENTS OF A STAPLE STORY

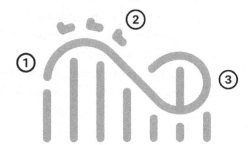

① The Before

Be as descriptive as possible. What emotion does this bring forth?

② The Ah-Ha

What moved you to: start a business, make a change, shift your perspective? Notice that little details create a visual for your audience and personalize the story.

③ The Who You Are Becoming

Although this is your story, you are showing them how they too can do it like you!

I want to point out that when you tell your Staple Story, you should be addressing a problem (or multiple problems) that your ideal customer/team member may have been through and describing how you personally wrestled with the problem, too. Then, you showcase the desire you had to change. In my case, I didn't directly state it, but it can be inferred from my Staple Story that I desired to lose weight, be in a community with other women, and live a life that allowed me to do more than just get by. And the solution to said problems? That's the picture you paint of "who you are becoming."

Below is a breakdown of my own Staple Story and the plot points that fall into each of the three categories above.

1. The "Before": From a distance, I watched my overly enthusiastic sorority sister talk about her work as a coach. I found myself getting curious about her work while I struggled with my own fitness goals, and I certainly didn't

have the same type of enthusiasm for grading papers as she did for fitness. At first I found her annoying, but I eventually got curious.

2. The "Ah-Ha": After months of watching her post about her workouts and her meal plans, and even buying a bootleg copy of Insanity from the internet, I finally reached out in what to her likely seemed a random message and inquired about what she did.

3. The "Who You Are Becoming": What started as a way to get the groceries paid for became a full-time direct sales career.

Check out this example of a client's Staple Story:

"Have you ever found yourself navigating a sea of uncertainty when finding the right products based on your needs? I want you to know that you ARE NOT alone. I had always prioritized taking care of my skin, but I was lost in a maze of guesswork when choosing the right products. I followed the trends, emulated what others were using, and hoped for the best.

Deep down, I knew I needed more. It was around the age of thirty-two when I began to notice subtle changes in my skin. The delicate web of wrinkles started to appear around my eyes, serving as a gentle reminder of the passage of time. I realized that it was time to step up my skincare game and seek a more informed approach.

I immersed myself in a wealth of knowledge and guidance, learning the importance of tailored skincare regimens and the transformative power of the right products. The Miracle Set became my faithful companion on this newfound path to radiant skin. As I diligently followed the steps of this skincare ritual, I started to witness a remarkable transformation.

The compliments began to pour in from friends and loved ones who took notice of the positive changes in my complexion. Their kind words echoed in my heart, reinforcing the belief that I was on the right track. As time passed and my journey with MK deepened, I decided to take things further. I upgraded to the Timewise Repair Set, a veritable superhero of anti-aging skincare systems. It felt like an armor of youthfulness, an arsenal of potent ingredients working in harmony to defy the signs of aging. To supercharge my routine, I introduced Retinol and boosters, unlocking new dimensions of rejuvenation. The results were astonishing, even to my own discerning eyes. I couldn't help but marvel at my skin's newfound luminosity and resilience.

To learn more about Mary Kay products, send me a message with the words 'MORE INFO' and let's chat!"

- Theresa LaCesa, Mary Kay

Anatomy of a Winning Staple Story on Social Media:
1. A strong tagline. This is the first sentence or statement seen by the viewer.
2. A relatable problem. This is how the reader connects to you.
3. Small details. Paint the picture of what it was actually like.
4. A clear turning point that addresses how the decision was made.
5. A picture of what can be possible for someone else.
6. A clear call to action.

Why Most Direct Sellers Fail at Storytelling (and What You Can Do About It)

I know it's nice and comfortable to believe the expression, "Everyone has a story," or, "Every story matters." But let me be clear that there is a strategy to telling a story that can move people to take action. Unlike fiction writing where we want to cheer on the hero, in marketing, we have to shift from being the hero to being the guide. In Donald Miller's book, *Building A StoryBrand: Clarify Your Message So Customers Will Listen*, he states, "Customers don't generally care about your story; they care about their own. Your customer should be the hero of your story, not your brand."[6]

So, if we are telling our own story, how do we make them care? So glad you asked! It's actually really simple, so simple that it's mind-blowing. Are you ready?

Define exactly what your customer wants and position yourself as the guide to help them get exactly what they want.

That's it. Simple, right? Winning in marketing is about solving a problem for your ideal customer. In order to show that person you can help them, you have to make their problem yours. I mentioned the TikTok celebrity's failed attempt at

---

6 Donald Miller, introduction to *Building a StoryBrand: Clarify Your Message So Customers Will Listen*, epub edition (Harper Collins Leadership, 2017), ix.

marketing to her audience at the beginning of this section. It failed because she was (and still is) the hero of her brand; she's not the guide. In order to avoid the same fate, we have to keep these two considerations at the forefront of our mind:

1. Do you care about me?
2. Can you actually help me?

We have to think like our customers. We have to think about how our content is being consumed by the person on the other side of the screen. We have to speak to our ideal team members and customers in a way that screams, "She wants me to win! It's like she's speaking right to me!" To do this, we must define what your customer or future team member wants:

Identify your ideal customer's/team member's problems. Sure, we can look at the surface-level problem we resolve (for example, if we sell face soap, we can talk about acne), but the deeper we go, the more our audience feels like they are being spoken to directly.

Using the face soap example, here's how to set a before that goes deeper: "When I was seventeen, my acne was so bad that I looked in the mirror and started connecting the dots on my face—partly out of boredom, but more because I wanted to see anything else but the acne—even if that meant Sharpie®. At least then I could hide."

Wow! This "before" is so much deeper than just, "I struggled with acne."

Identify your ideal customer's/team member's desires. What does someone stand to gain by using the services you offer? I see so many direct sellers highlighting the wins, but I want to challenge you to speak to the bigger desire.

Let's take that same example from above again. A great "after" moment might sound something like: "I was running out the door, late as usual, to the MOPS meeting, when I caught my reflection in the rearview mirror as I was making sure that the diaper bag was in the back seat. It hit me—my reflection. It was without a blemish or a bump, save for a few beautiful lines and some fading scars that told the story of what once was. There in the rearview mirror was a fresh-faced thirty-something, without makeup and with confidence her teenage self could only dream of."

Now, imagine being a woman on the other side of the screen reading this narrative and seeing her own acne scars, imagining the almost impossible: going out of the home without makeup.

Demonstrating the specific solution you offer. In the coming sections, we will talk more about how to sell without coming off as salesy, but I want to remind you that we cannot be afraid to sell. Too often, I hear these amazing stories from network marketers with powerful messages and transformations, and yet they shy away from selling. *Listen, sister. If people don't know you are open for business, then you aren't running a business. You're playing around on a social media account.*

So, we tell a story. We frame ourselves as a guide, we get to the heart of our prospects' problems and their actual desires, and then give them an actual solution. Easy, right? Absolutely!

So, your next question is likely, "How long is this going to take?" My question in response is, "How long have you got?"

How Long Does This Actually Take?

Becoming the guide for your ideal customer takes time. There's no skirting around it. It's a process. So, when it comes to your content, I want you to remember this: *If you sound like a broken record, you're doing it right.* You will have to tell both versions (business and product) of your story often. In fact, one of the biggest takeaways I hope you receive from my personal Staple Story (how I started in direct sales) is this: it's going to take time. I've shared the red pen story so many times that people started to know it as the story of the girl who doesn't do road trips without Combos. It isn't an accident that people picked up on the small details like the road trip snacks or the red pen I held while grading papers. It was a relatable detail that allowed my potential team members to feel seen and heard. It drew a connection. It isn't an accident that many of my team members were teachers and they all knew the importance of really great road trip snacks.

My audience heard the story multiple times through multiple posts with multiple calls to action. Many of them saw the post *more than once* (or twice, or three, four, five times) before they took action. But they each saw a bit of their own story in mine.

It's going to be easy to post a Staple Story and then cross your fingers, hoping to sign your ideal customer or your ideal team member. But it's more like planting a seed and continuing to water the seed until you see growth. Here are a few things you can do:

- Repeat yourself. Don't assume that everyone has heard your Staple Story! The reason it's called a "staple" is because it's your go-to content for connecting with your ideal customer and team member.
- Add the little details because they make a big difference. Small details in your story often create a connection between you and your potential team member/customer. Provide details that make the visual of your story pop! (Think about that red pen and those Combos!)
- Provide a clear call to action in your content. It's great to tell your story but be clear about what you want people to do with your story. Drop a comment? Click a link?
- Give them a reason to want to read your Staple Story. Start with a strong hook that makes your reader feel included and excited to hear more!

Chapter Eight

Years ago, one of my first jobs was waiting tables at Bob Evans®. That's right; Rise and Shine Breakfast with a side of biscuits and gravy was my specialty. I would wake up around 5 am for the first shift, and although my early mornings at Bob Evans didn't last more than a couple of years, I learned a lot from the early shift waitresses who knew how to maximize their tip potential and increase their table turnover.

"Oh, you want the Rise and Shine Breakfast? Great! How about a glass of orange juice with that? Have you tried our banana bread? No? It's heavenly! Perhaps a loaf to go would be great?"

And table turnovers? I was the queen of serving my customers well, serving them quickly, and helping the bussers flip tables to keep the line moving—in my direction.

So, when I decided to take on a new waitressing position at a more upscale restaurant that served homemade Italian dishes and toted a weekend dinner wait time of well over two hours, I applied my Bob Evans skill set and blew the minds of my fellow employees with my nightly tip earnings.

"You know what wine goes amazing with that dish? The cabernet. It's a must. Would you prefer the bottle?" "Listen, I know I am preparing to put this order in, but at full disclosure, the chocolate cheesecake is to die for and there are only two slices left. Do you want me to add that to your order now?"

My point is this: Skill sets are transferable. I gained a ton of knowledge of how to work hard and maximize income potential by working in the service industry, and I applied it to direct sales. In Section Four, I discuss exceptional customer service in detail, but those in the industry who are crushing their goals are also strategic with the service.

My experience in the food industry and knowing why people buy came in handy as I began a direct sales business. I learned then that people were willing to purchase from me because they trusted me. I gave them the inside scoop about the chocolate cheesecake, and I knew the best cabernet that would go with their Italian entrée selection! But likeability alone won't close your sales.

My sales as a server increased because I was there to give each diner a unique dining experience (not just bring out their food). Likewise, in direct sales, I closed sales because the content I created on my social media became an experience for others. And, deep breaths, what I am about to say (and likely repeat over and over to the point of sounding like a broken record) is this: *Your brand isn't about you. It's about what you can do for someone else.*

I know. I realize you are the author of your story. The content has to be about you, but your audience pays your bills, and if you want them to pay those bills, you have to give them a reason to give you their money. Please, hear me. Don't take that out of context! Let's not skirt around the fact that you are spending time on social media. It's a promotional tool, and if we aren't careful, we can fall into this trap of posting personal content that doesn't do anything for our potential customers and team members. If that's the case, we are wasting our time.

People have to believe that purchasing from you is a worthwhile investment, whether you sell protein shakes, leisure wear, or skincare. They will not purchase from you if they do not know what you can do for them. So, the content you write about yourself isn't meant to serve you. (Hint: This is the chapter where I address what most people are doing wrong and what most well-meaning uplines are teaching wrong.) Here's what your audience is really wondering:

1. Why should I care about your content?
2. How will what you share make my life better?
3. How can I trust you?
4. Do you really care about me?

I'll say it again. Your brand isn't about you. It's about what you can do for someone else.

Let me tell you a quick story about two photographers. The first photographer posts, "Family photo session: $400. Booking now!" The second photographer posts, "Don't miss it. Capture the laughter and joy of the moments that will be gone too fast. $1,000. Booking now!" Which photographer books more clients? If you guessed the second one, you're right. Here's why. The first photographer takes pictures. The second photographer creates an experience that addresses the desire to create an unforgettable opportunity to capture laughter and joy. The first photographer and the second photographer were both attempting to close sales, but the second photographer understood the sale was about speaking to the needs of the customer.

Does your content speak to the needs of your ideal customer or team member?

If you feel like I am speaking right to you, it's time to roll up your sleeves and get to work! Are you ready to see what selfless, audience-first marketing looks like?

First, let me introduce you to a direct seller's best friend, the niche content trifecta: your passion, your knowledge, and your profit.

DISCOVERING YOUR NICHE

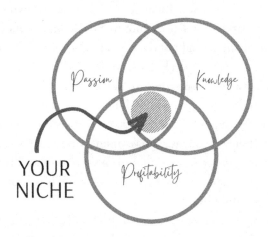

Passion

To start, can I talk about a personal beef for a minute? It's the word "passion." It's thrown around like confetti.

"I am passionate about building a business."

"I am passionate about building a life of freedom."

"I am passionate about helping others succeed."

"I am passionate about homemade cheeseburgers."

I could create a book on the misuse of the word "passion." But instead of a book, let's devote only a moment to rewriting our definition of passion (just so we're all on the same page).

Passion (noun), def.:

Intense, driving, or overmastering feelings of conviction or an outbreak of anger.

Passion is a conviction. Passion isn't just what you care immensely about. There's also an element of passion derived from anger.

What does this look like? So glad you asked. Years ago, when I was throwing around the word passion like beads at Mardi Gras to describe my business, I was stuck wondering how to do my work differently. Every other distributor in my wellness company was passionate about fitness or passionate about helping people. I had no idea what made me different until I attended a leadership conference.

The speaker at the conference revisited the word "passion," sharing that it should make you uncomfortable. He had us close our eyes and took us on a visualization practice. "Imagine this," he said. "Imagine you are driving down the highway and you find your mind wandering. Pause. Your first thoughts are of course the kids or your to-do list. Maybe the thought of the Crockpot™—you can't quite remember if you turned it on. Pause. Before you know it, your mind wanders deeper. Your body tenses as you recollect a time of discomfort. You try to break concentration, but it's as if your mind wants you to stay there. Before you know it, your eyes are swelling with tears. Maybe you're angry. Maybe you're overwhelmingly grateful. Maybe you're scared. But wherever you are, you've unknowingly arrived at your passion."

Passion, you see, cannot just be a word thrown around like confetti. It's an overwhelming feeling that consumes your thoughts and leaves you with an energy that forces you to do something.

That day, during the visualization activity, I was overcome with a wave of powerful anger. Fresh in my mind was a friend (only thirty-two years old) who had passed away from cancer. She passed away; I lived. My mind wandered to thoughts of cancer: the disease, the process of misdiagnosis, the anger of having my concerns be brushed aside because I was healthy, the trauma of living when others didn't, the fact that my workouts in the morning started with gratitude for having my feet on the ground and an intense desire to help others take responsibility for their health because it mattered, and the thought that if you had the ability to sweat, you should sweat for those who could not. I had just met my passion.

A few months later, a social media movement known as "Every. Sweat. Matters." was created. On that day I started to own passion as more than just a word but as a conviction. The movement went on to raise well over $100K for various non-profits, not to mention the impact the movement had on others taking ownership of their health. My personal and team recruitment goals skyrocketed, and my sales grew significantly.

I say all of this not to brag but to share that when you own the uncomfortable part of your passion, you can begin to own that conviction. Passion stops just being a word and turns into a fierce desire to do something with it.

How can you do the same?

I am a firm believer that you should take note of your thoughts when they wander and check in with where they go. They usually go to the places we don't want them to travel, but there's a lot of open space to explore what those thoughts actually mean. I'm including a few questions for you to journal to give you some room to form deeper thoughts.

1. What's been a common theme throughout your life? What do many people say about you? What do you often think of yourself?
2. People closest to you say you are so good at _____.
3. What do people often seek your insight on? What do people often want your opinion about?
4. If money wasn't an option, what service would you provide free of charge?
5. Looking at your weekly calendar, what gets you the most excited?
6. What gets your blood boiling? What's a problem in the world that you feel pulled to fix?
7. What topics do you have a hard time holding back on?

Now that we have a clear understanding of our passion, let's intersect our passion with our knowledge.

Knowledge

A list of things I know absolutely nothing about:

- Math that involves letters. There have been multiple tearful, tantrum-filled occasions around our kitchen table when it comes to algebra homework—mostly my own tears, but there it is.
- My husband's inability to relax on a rare Saturday when we have nothing going on. Hence why there are multiple home renovations happening at one time that never quite seem to get done.
- Why the scale seems to move when my husband merely thinks of losing weight, and why the scale seems to vehemently refuse to move in the direction of my goals after months of trying to lose weight. Kind of unfair if you ask me, but whatever.

Things I know an annoyingly obscene amount about:

- Overcoming self-limiting beliefs and helping others overcome theirs too.
- Tricking my children into cleaning their rooms.
- Plot development, writing, and marketing.

Most people realize they know a lot about a little. It never ceases to amaze me how much random information I've hoarded over the years. But what most people don't realize is that they probably know a good deal about something that others are looking to learn more about. We often get confused about the word "expert," disqualifying ourselves as industry leaders (yes, I said industry leaders) because we don't think we know enough, or we don't have enough time in the industry, or we see someone else who is further along. But when it comes to knowledge, establishing credibility comes from a desire to keep learning and sharing the knowledge you've received along the way. As a direct seller, your job isn't to have it all figured out. Your job is to share your knowledge as you go.

When mentoring women through the Chic Branding Experience, one of the first questions I like to ask is, "What do you enjoy learning and researching?" Their answers often fascinate me. I've worked with brand owners who love exploring everything from hormonal health to causes of autism to origins of the dinosaurs to homeschooling and skin care and weight loss and enhancing marriages and overcoming trauma. People fascinate me with their knowledge. But what never fails to blow my mind is that most people I work with think that they're boring.

"I'm just a mom." "I'm just a coach." "I'm just navigating a recent divorce."

Can we have a chat? Come in close, because I want you to know something. I want you to believe with your entire being what I am about to throw down.

You are not *just* anything. You are an exceptional human with interests that have grown because of your personal experiences, and your knowledge may be someone else's starting point.

 Scan the QR code to learn more about The Chic Branding Experience!

Did you know that the chances of you being born who you are is estimated to be about 1 in 400 trillion? From the moment of conception, a complex sequence of events unfolds that leads to the formation of a unique human being, with its own set of genetic traits, personality, and experiences. There's nothing just about you. Imagine for a second if you saw yourself the way others see you. Imagine for a moment if you showed up believing that the 1 in 400 trillion chance of you even being born was for a unique purpose.

I get it. It's hard to wrap my head around it, too. But part of what makes us unique is how our experiences have shaped our own knowledge.

As humans, we all have an unsatiated thirst for knowledge—to understand and to be understood. The things you care about—that you want to spend time learning about, that you stay up late wondering about, that get you out of bed excited to start your day—all of those things are clues to how you can better serve the people around you.

So, let's start with a few quick questions for you to think about. When it comes to your interests and what you know about, don't limit yourself to what you sell. For example, if you are in the skincare industry, don't limit your knowledge base to only skincare. Instead, think about everything you've learned over the course of your lifetime and what you love talking about. Oh, see how I am already preparing you to connect it back to passion?!

- What do you love researching?
- What topics at a party spark your interest?
- What type of books or audiobooks do you love reading?
- What topics do your friends seek your advice on?
- What was your favorite class in high school or trade school or college?
- Who do you follow on social media that doesn't have anything to do with what you sell?
- Who do you find simply fascinating? Why?
- What life experiences have piqued your interest in specific topics?
- What topics could you comfortably and lovingly debate with others?
- What brings you energy and excitement?

The things you care about aren't accidental, and the things you have foundational knowledge about are influenced by your personal life experiences. But here's what we have to be aware of: We can vastly underestimate our own knowledge because we believe we aren't equipped to share or qualified to give others advice.

When it comes to knowledge, no one is more of an expert on you than you. Our experiences and our persistence to learn, to grow, and to evolve are part of the human experience. You are a human experiencing life in your own unique way—a way that doesn't need a college degree or a certificate of completion.

But we need to be honest about how we share our experiences (almost a disclaimer of sorts). When I spoke of my knowledge about losing twenty-five pounds with the products I used, I often shared, "I am not a nutritionist, a fitness expert, or a dietician. I am a mom who lost twenty-five pounds when she started to get curious about making small changes to her lifestyle. Here is what I learned through making those small changes…" That is the power of being one step ahead.

So, we've talked about passion and knowledge, and while those two things can create a great brand, as direct sellers we have to let people know that we are open for business. We have to make sure that the things that light us up and the knowledge we've acquired through our experiences intersect with how we can make a profit.

Profit

Imagine with me for a minute that you are preparing to open the doors to your brick-and-mortar business. Let's say it's a small coffee and clothing boutique. You have been preparing for months, making sure all the small details are worked out. The coffee offers a variety of flavors and the clothing boutique is stocked with the hottest trends. You've visualized it for months. On opening day, the masses start lining up at the door. But then the nerves hit. "What if the coffee machine breaks? What if no one purchases the clothing?" So, instead of opening the doors, you decide you need just one more week, until everything is perfect. Then the next week comes, more people are lined up, but the nerves hit hard again and you just aren't ready … it's not the right time. It happens again, and again, and again.

You keep the doors to your business closed, hidden behind a pretty window display and coffee that's gone cold.

Friend, this is what most direct sellers are doing with their social media. They are creating content that is trending, keeping up with what others in the industry are doing, and doing anything for the likes and the engagement, but never stopping to ask, "Do people know the doors to my business are actually open?"

Here's where I wish, gosh I wish, we were sitting across from each other so that I could remind you of one of the most important, often overlooked details. People will not know about your business unless you talk about your business. People won't know that you are open for business if you don't create content about your business. People won't know about how they can be served by your business unless you show them proof that you are there to serve them.

It's simple. You have to talk about your business. You have to market your products. You have to market your business opportunity. You cannot assume that your audience knows how amazing your offer is!

And here's the kicker: at first it's going to feel weird—especially if you're not used to talking about it. You may fumble over your words like a third-string receiver in the Super Bowl. You may feel a little awkward at first, but the more you do it, the easier and more natural it becomes.

But How Do I Avoid the Ick Factor?

We all know the ick factor. We all know what it's like to be on the receiving end of a well-intentioned, end-of-the-month message asking for a sale. We all know what it's like to see an account blasting stock photos of sales, limited-time offers, and going-going-gone products. This won't be you, not anymore. Instead, we are going to apply the Unique Sharing Proposition to your work.

Unique Sharing Proposition, def.

Your unique approach to the product, services, and experience that you offer.

To identify your USP (Unique Sharing Proposition) we have to examine what you do and who you are. Below are a few specific questions to help you identify your USP.

Questions that relate to what you do:
- What is the problem that YOU can resolve for your customer/followers? (connect to your product/service/experience)
- What problem can your product/service resolve?
- What desires do you help your ideal customer achieve?
- How do you serve your customers differently?
- What makes the experience for your customers or team unique from others in your industry?

Questions that relate to who you are:
- What do you enjoy learning and researching?
- What topics do you naturally bring up in conversation?
- What do your friends often ask for your advice about?
- What types of communities are you involved in?
- Who are you outside of what you do?

It always fascinates me how the many women I've worked with through the Chic Branding Experience can approach things differently. Although many of them may sell the same products, *none* of them should approach their products or the opportunity in the same way. *Not one.* It's like this: when you speak to everyone, you speak to no one! So, let's put down the megaphone and start clearly speaking to the people right in front of us—the women who most need what you have to offer.
- Identify why you are doing what you do.

- How do you do it slightly differently from others?
- Who benefits most from working with you?

Why does this all matter? Because now…
- You will always be clear on who you serve and why.
- You can pinpoint exactly who you speak to.
- You can identify what makes them tick.
- You can serve them exactly where they are.
- You can determine whom you do not serve.
- You will speak directly to your target, letting them feel heard.
- You will know what language they use and tailor content to where they are in their purchasing journey.
- You can tailor additional products and services to meet their needs, creating life-long customers.

The deeper the answers to these questions, the clearer your USP becomes!

The Undeniable "Find Your Niche Formula"

When you have a clear understanding of your knowledge, your passion, and how you profit (through the products as well as the opportunity), you begin to clarify your specific niche. No one can do business quite like you, and no one can provide the same experience to the direct sales business that you can. With a clear understanding of your niche, your content should speak to your ideal customer/ team member's current struggles and desires and provide them with a plausible solution. The key is creating content that serves well.

I don't know how many customer avatar trainings I've listened to over the course of eleven years, but really, finding your niche is simple. The key is to not overthink it.

Passion + Knowledge + Profit = Niche. That's it. That's the message.

Identify your passion. Connect it to your knowledge. Bring it back to how you serve through your products and your opportunity, and you have found your niche. No avatar training is required.

In 2012, one of the first marketing posts that I wrote had an image of my products and the cryptic words, "Decide. Commit. Succeed," followed by a hyperlink to purchase a starter kit. Needless to say, no one purchased my product on that day, and for the weeks that followed, it seemed that I was just not cut out for this whole network marketing thing. It took me an absurd amount of time to realize that people didn't want a link (not yet anyway). I needed time to establish my credibility by serving my audience well. Posting a link with a few words and crossing my fingers that someone would sign up wasn't a successful business strategy. As I started to get curious about what drove people to ask questions, what made people comment on my posts, and how I could be different in the industry, I realized it all had a lot to do with niche (passion, knowledge, and profit). What drew people to learn more was the unique way that I served them. Interestingly enough, the more I served, the more I sold.

In the next chapter, let's walk through what building an intentional brand looks like and how to take the first steps in breaking up with your personal brand (yes, I am asking you to stop building a personal brand. I know, mind-blowing!)

Shall we move on to how to actually serve so that you can sell?

I, Me, My

It's been approximately 6,327 days since I've been on a first date. So, I may be a little rusty on how it all works, but I imagine it goes something like this …

- Your date opens the car door. Check.
- Tells you that you look nice. Check.
- Opens the door while gently touching the small of your back. PURRR…
- Tells a terrible joke to break up the awkwardness. Little inappropriate, but kind of funny. Check.
- Can't seem to put his phone down during dinner. Red flag.
- Spends the entire dinner talking about himself. Okay, bye.

Do those rules still apply? Like I said, I'm a little rusty on the whole dating game, but I can tell you that I am familiar with the psychology of a sale, and to be honest it's not too different from the dating game.

When it comes to direct sales, if there's not a connection, there's not going to be a sale. So, let's say for a minute that you're on the hunt for a skincare solution. There are so many options out there. You've tried a few finds from the local beauty counter, but it's left your skin dry and patchy. You remember that girl on Instagram, the one who's always giving you tons of tips on how to have a more youthful glow. You go to her account. You scroll through to see if she can solve your problem:

- She sells some type of skincare. Check.
- Her own skin looks amazing. Check.
- She shows her before and after. Wow.
- She talks about herself over and over and over again in her content. Eh.
- You don't see any proof outside of her own testimonial that the products work. Red flag.
- She never comes out and says what she does, so you find yourself going down a rabbit hole to figure out if she can actually help you. Okay, bye.

We have become so saturated by the message of self that we've forgotten the key driver of sales comes through serving.

In Chapter Seven, we examined the Staple Story. We talked about how to make our story less about us and more about the person reading our story. The audience-first marketing approach forces us to create content that's for our audience, not for us. Since we have to share more than a Staple Story through our content, we have to think *intentionally* about who is on the receiving end of our message. Think of it like this:

Intentional Brand

A brand that showcases your personality as well as how you serve others. The goal of the content is to help your audience understand how you serve uniquely, what they stand to gain by working with you, and ultimately what makes you different from others in the industry.

Personal Brand

A brand that showcases your personality.

Why are we moving away from personal brands and into intentional brands? Because people don't care about you. They care about what you can do for them.

People are selective with who they follow because they want to know what's in it for them. We used to be really interested in *Keeping Up with the Kardashians*, and now, as we find more distractions vying for our attention, we can be selective. We don't want to follow just to follow. We want to follow accounts and brands that do something for us, that align with our personal values and make us better in some way.

There's no feeling lukewarm about brands that move us to take action.

There's an old Toby Keith song (yes, I may be aging myself) where he talked about a doomed relationship with a woman. It starts off okay, but before too long she's driving him crazy because she won't stop talking about herself.

"I wanna talk about me, wanna talk about I

Wanna talk about number one, oh my, me my"

When I mentor my Chic Branding Experience coaching clients, the very first thing I do is look at their most recent nine posts and ask myself the question:

"How many of the nine posts contain the words 'I, me, my' in the first sentence?" And I know what you are doing right now—go on. Go look. How much of your content is about you? Which brings me to the second question. "How many of the last nine posts contain the word 'we'?"

Inclusive writing is a way to put yourself and your reader into the writing. It's time to take a deep breath, look at your content, and ask yourself, "Who am I talking about?" Are you serving the best highlights of your life, or are you showing up to serve the person on the other side of the screen?

I started teaching three types of perspectives that direct sellers use as content writers. Take a moment to read over the three common perspectives and ask yourself which one you use most in your own content:

Pit Dweller: This writer most often tells the audience what their problem is by pointing the finger at them and telling others what they need to change. You get a feeling that this writer isn't very confident in themselves and much of their content is regurgitated. There's often an inconsistency, and it's hard to feel connected to this writer because you feel like they often call you out.

Trench Leader: This type of writer speaks from experience by sharing personal testimonials and real-life examples. She often uses the word "we," making her readers feel included within the content. She positions herself as a leader who wants to do business right alongside you, together.

Lincoln Navigator: This type of writer speaks from past experience. You get the feeling that this leader is confident in her ability to lead her customers and distributors to success. You don't always feel connected to this speaker personally, but you are often motivated by her. She positions herself as an experienced guide, ready to help you on your way.

Disclaimer: I would go so far as to say about 85 percent of direct sellers don't think about how their writing is being experienced by the reader (yes, even some industry leaders with massive followings). It's not your fault. We've been so saturated with the message of self that it feels somewhat unnatural for us to talk about someone else's problems, desires, or ultimately how we provide a solution. It's a lot easier to hide behind ourselves than it is to step up as an industry leader who can help other people get results. But *do not* worry. With a little tough love and a lot of mistakes (have I mentioned that I haven't always done direct sales right?) I can show you how to not just create followers (please know this is never going to be the primary goal here at *Direct Sales Done Right*), but rather how to support your loyal followers so they become lovers of your products and members of your team.

Let me add another quick disclaimer. I really stink at sugarcoating. I try, I really do, but I'd rather just cut to the chase, shoot straight, and help you get right to work. You in? Here's what you need to consider before you post content!

1. Create purposeful content that serves your audience. Ask yourself, how do I want the reader on the other side of the screen to experience my content? What do I want them to do with the content?
2. Ask yourself if your content serves or sells.

3. Create content that promotes your opportunity and your products but don't expect the content to "invite" for you.
4. Show energy and empathy for your audience. Have energy and enthusiasm for what you do, and how you do it differently, but have empathy for the struggle they may be currently experiencing.

It isn't about you.

Let's play a game. Which one of the following scenarios best describes you:

1. You signed up for the direct sales opportunity and became the poster child of the A+ student. Not only are you consistently posting but you aren't afraid to sell. A quick look at your platform and err'body knows exactly what company you are a part of, and that you LOVE what you do. What you struggle to understand is why conversion is so hard?
2. You signed up for the direct sales opportunity, but you don't have a background in selling. You often wonder how anyone actually has time to always be "on." And you absolutely—ABSOLUTELY—refuse to be one of those direct sellers who never seem to shut up about what they have to offer. You have no problem having conversations with people privately, and you definitely invite! What you struggle to understand is why conversion is so hard?
3. You signed up for the direct sales opportunity and have learned how to talk about the products and the opportunity. You've grown a nice little following, and you have no problem with consistency. In fact, a lot of your content gets great reach and engagement. You'll market your products and the opportunity. But something is missing. You're doing all the things. What you struggle to understand is why conversion is so hard?

Which one sounds most familiar to you? Maybe it's a little of each of them? Here's what I can tell you (this will for sure make you feel better). The majority of direct sellers find themselves in categories one, two, and/or three. Yes, that means *most* of the women and men in this industry are often questioning, "Why isn't this converting?" So, here's what you need to know about why your content isn't converting...

It isn't your fault. Ah, doesn't that feel good to know you're not alone? Well, hold up. You are not off the hook yet. What's the expression? "When you know better, you do better." Yep, that's the one. What did I say about doing *Direct Sales Done Right?*

Listen friend, if the majority of people in the industry aren't doing it quite right (no, this is not a call out), no wonder the industry gets a bad rep! But we are committed to getting this right, and it's actually easier than you think. Why? Because when we make it our mission to confidently serve over selling, we do better.

Here's where we start to do better!

The B.E.S. Practices for Direct Sales Content Creation

I really tried to make the acronym work out for the B.E.S.T., but there didn't seem to be a need to add a letter and cause confusion. So, let's focus on the B.E.S. instead of B.E.S.T. Practices for Direct Sales Content Creation.

As a direct seller, we have to create content for our audience. People crave honesty, simplicity, and consistency. The good news is, we aren't creating Kardashian-style content where people feel like they need to keep up for the sake of—well, geez, does anyone know *why* they need to keep up with the Kardashians?! Instead, we are creating content for our audience—content that serves them, content that excites them, and content that is designed to help them take action. Here's what my clever little acronym actually stands for:

- Brand Awareness: You are making people aware of how you do business differently than others in your industry and other similar industries. It's more INTENTIONAL than PERSONAL.
- Engagement: You serve your audience with content that is entertaining, value-add, and usually somewhat binge-worthy so it elicits engagement.
- Sales: This is the content that educates your audience on the current problem they may be experiencing and the desire they have, and ultimately provides a solution you can offer!

Brand Awareness

At the beginning of this chapter, we discussed building an intentional brand over a personal brand. In order to do this, we need to clarify exactly how we do business differently.

When I was starting in direct sales, I remember being taught the well-meaning advice to, "Never post anything political, controversial, or anything that could be deemed as offensive."

Well, well, well. Well-meaning advice, I failed you. Who you are, the values you hold, and the beliefs you have are part of what makes you unique. In a world that is so focused on being liked, is it wild to think that maybe trying to be liked by everyone is what's preventing you from being seen?

I have three *key* questions that have allowed me to move into a space of not being liked by many but being impactful to a few. Impact, after all, drives sales. The key questions to ask yourself when you post are:

1. Is this content helpful?
2. Is this content hopeful?
3. Is this content healing?

If the answer is yes to one or all of these questions, then you are building a brand in alignment with who you are. If the answer is no, allow yourself to wrestle with why you want to post it.

Guess what? Many times I don't post the content I am considering because ultimately I know it's not going to serve my audience.

So, what does this look like? A few years ago, I didn't want to share my faith publicly because I felt that it was more of a private thing, until the world got wild, and the less I talked about it, the *more* I wrestled with my line of work. Now, I talk about how my faith is my first business, not supporting direct sellers. I talk about prioritizing God over business. I talk about the things God has done through my work, and you know what? It's *not* for everyone (to clarify, God is for everyone, but I am not). And that is okay!

Similarly, I have friends with strong political views and strong social justice views. Listen, if it's part of who you are and the content you provide can be helpful, hopeful, or healing, then you can either hide from it or you can embrace it and become more of who you are supposed to be.

This past week, I had a conversation with a friend who shared with me that a recent post was met with a number of direct messages claiming that she was "out of touch with reality" and "rude for assuming that everyone wanted her lifestyle." Instead of letting her spiral down the rabbit hole of, "I am not meant to do this," I asked her three questions:

1. Was your post intended to be helpful?
2. Was your post intended to be hopeful?
3. Was your post intended to be healing?

She responded "yes" to two out of three. Then I asked her, "Did you show up with energy and empathy?" Her response was, "I think so!"

My response to her and you is, "KEEP GOING!!!" Friend, not everyone is going to like you. Not everyone is going to need your services. Not everyone is going to want what you have to offer. And this is where you can take a deep breath because that's okay.

It's like this: You could have the best coffee in the world (Black Rifle shout out!), rich with bold and vibrant hints of caramel and a soft aroma that immediately brings you back to memories of slow Saturday mornings under your oversized blankie. But you and I both know, no matter what you say or how much you love your coffee, there are still people who don't drink coffee. Two of those people happen to be my best friends. I don't understand it. I don't really like it. I believe that all people can change. But, you know, no one is perfect. All joking aside, my point is this: Not everyone is going to be okay with you or what you share. My question is, are you okay with being you? Are you okay with someone not approving of you or what you do?

There's this saying, "You can be the ripest, juiciest peach in the world, and there's still going to be somebody who hates peaches." Not everyone is going to like you, but *you* need to like you.

Your Intentions

*STRONG VIEW (Please skip if you are easily offended):

People are already judging you. They are. People make assumptions. People have opinions. But some of those judgments being made are by the people who are consuming your content and experiencing what it's like to work with you *long* before you ever make the sale. So, one of the best questions to ask yourself is, "What do you want that experience to look like for someone else?"

To be honest, at first, I wanted to play it safe. I was good with people feeling lukewarm about me. But indifference isn't the best conversion strategy. I was just scared. I was partly scared to share my faith because I thought I was "Jesus-ing wrong." I was scared to share some of my conservative views, afraid that someone would be offended. Then I went to therapy, and I thought about that lukewarm faucet, and I thought about how I just don't want anyone feeling lukewarm about me. I'd rather a few people tell me how I *fire them up* than listen to the likes of those drowning in the chilliness of my watered-down content.

Some of the best advice I ever received from my time in therapy (heck yes, I am a huge believer in the power of prayer *and* the power of therapy), which still remains some of the best advice I've ever gotten and is something I've carried with me throughout building multiple businesses is this: ***It's a choice to be offended.***

It hits kind of hard, right? In a culture that's so quick to cancel, to unfollow, and to be offended, I've found that some of the most influential mentors in my life are the ones I don't agree with. You see, if we aren't careful when we find ourselves offended, it can force us to be incredibly defensive. Right?! And since I feel I can let my guard down here, I might as well share that this week I found myself offended.

I found myself hurt by someone in my life, by someone who has some very bold beliefs—beliefs that are quite different from mine. It was easy to be offended. It was easier to be hurt. And wow, it was easy to see that hurt spiral to anger and then to resentment. But do you know what's interesting about being offended? It's a choice. It was my choice to believe her intention was to hurt instead of believing that she herself was hurting. It was my choice to believe that she should do better and be better instead of believing she was actually just doing her best.

It was my choice to forgive her—not for her sake, but for mine. But it was also my choice to consider what she was saying and ask myself, "Why am I offended by this?"

For what it's worth, believing everyone is doing their best changes things. And knowing that everyone's best looks different means we don't need to be offended but empathetic. Apply the belief that everyone, even if you feel hurt by their words or actions, is just doing their best, and you begin to see your perspective and your peace change.

Engagement

"I just don't get it. My followers are going up. I am still seeing a significant reach in my content, but my conversion is terrible! Can you help?"

One second, let me get my superhero cape, because I am about to rescue you from the engagement trap! Let's have a quick chat about one of my clients with over 170,000 followers. She's a direct seller who's branded herself as a busy mom of four who makes funny reels with her husband. And I will be the first to admit, I've binged her content at length; it's good! But I knew right away what was preventing her from seeing an increase in her sales and conversion to team members. As a content creator, she was known for humor, but she wasn't known as a leader in her industry. My client was creating engagement content without considering her marketing goals. GULP.

It's hard to believe that this woman with a massive following was struggling with confidence in her business, but our conversation revealed that she just didn't know how to talk about her work. She was struggling to connect the dots for her audience. And friend, it happens all the time. Engagement content is meant to support your marketing goals through serving, cultivating a community, and segueing into what you offer, but if you aren't sure how it connects back to what you market, you are wasting your time. It doesn't matter how big your following is if they don't know your business is open.

Yours truly wrestled with this very concept. When I created Chic Influencer a few years ago, I was becoming known for my humorous cancer reels and my marriage reels. My followers were increasing daily and my engagement was through the roof. Great, right? Wrong. I couldn't convert my followers to my services because I didn't prime them for my offers. They knew me as the girl who shared about her cancer experience and who created relatable marriage reels, but it didn't lead to sales—and wasn't that why I was spending time on social media?! Listen, I am not here to tell you that engagement doesn't matter (it does!) But I am here to tell you that it's not *everything*. Your engagement content is priming your audience for what you have to offer because they are experiencing your personality and your values. They are beginning to see your unique potential differently from others in the industry.

The sky's the limit with engagement content. However, my best advice is to keep it simple. You are going to want to consistently speak about the same thing over and over. (Yes, you may feel like you are a broken record, but I assure you that you are doing it right!) However, as you evolve, you may find that your content does as well. It's okay to "date" engagement content ideas for a bit before committing. See how specific content makes you feel as the creator and continue testing it out. Pay attention to how people respond, if it drives engagement that you feel excited about, and if it lends itself to a natural segue into what you do!

Sales

Alright, so we've learned that if Toby Keith's song, *I Wanna Talk About Me*, is on repeat in our content, then we likely need to make an adjustment. The quickest way to audit our own account is to make sure we have brand awareness content, engagement content, and sales (marketing) content.

Here's where you and I need to have a conversation about marketing styles. I find that there are usually two types of people:

1. The woman who LOVES her products and doesn't stop talking about them.
2. The woman who LOVES her products but is too scared to talk about them.

The same goes for the direct selling opportunity, but let's start by talking about the products. The healthiest place to be is in between the two examples above. We don't want to be the friendly kiosk worker in the mall chasing people down for sales, but we don't want to be the business that never has any customers in the store, causing you to question if it's actually open. People buy from those they trust. Your brand awareness content and your engagement content lay the foundation, but your sales content needs to address the problem your potential customer is experiencing, the desires they have, and why your services offer a solution. So, why do people buy? What makes your offer so enticing? According to a 2019 Edelman study, 81 percent of consumers say their ability to trust a brand to do what is right is a deciding factor or deal-breaker in their buying decisions.[7]

Common motives for buying:

- Financial Gain: they believe that a purchase or a decision to join your team will financially benefit them.
- Need: your prospect believes that you, your products, or your opportunity can resolve a problem.
- Health: Your prospect is wanting to live well and longer.
- Impulse: The prospect purchases out of excitement or urgency. You've given them a clear reason to take action!
- Pleasure: Although the prospect may not see the sale as essential, they want to indulge themselves.
- Fear: One of the most powerful tactics used in marketing because it applies to most situations, not just sales. It creates a sense of urgency and highlights a deficit that a prospect may be experiencing.
- Self-Improvement: When a prospect sees you as an authority in an area he or she would like to improve in, it appeals to the desire to change more than to stay the same.

Now, take a highlighter or make a note of which of these motives you speak to through your content. How'd you do? Is there variety? Or could you speak to a few of them more often? If we aren't giving people a reason to purchase based on their motives, we are missing the mark.

---

7 Niki Hall, "Four Core Elements Of Building A Trusted Brand," *Forbes*, July 1, 2022, https://www.forbes.com/sites/forbescommunicationscouncil/2022/07/01/four-core-elements-of-building-a-trusted-brand/

Connecting the Dots

Engagement content is meant to cultivate a comeback audience because they know that there's something in it for them. *Engagement content is giving people a clear reason to come back. Brand awareness is giving them a reason to stick around and sales content tells them exactly what's in it for them.* You need all three! So, take some time to reflect on content that is "showcasing" what you offer, how you offer it, and ask yourself, "Where can I make a connection?"

In your engagement content, can you naturally talk about what you have to offer? Is there an opportunity for conversation to start in the comments section?

In your sales content, can you share a case study that reveals a unique spin on how you serve your customers? Perhaps a weekly email or a complementary getting started call?

In your brand awareness content, can you incorporate a topic (like marriage, mom humor, gardening tips, cleaning hacks) that doesn't necessarily have anything to do with what you offer, but gives people a feel for what it's like to be served by you?

Quick story … I was really afraid to share the business opportunity. I was scared of being judged. I was scared that I would offend others, so I held tight to the belief that if someone wants to know more, they will ask. After all, I was showing the products. I was consistently posting. But the business? That made me nervous. So, I avoided it, or I would post about it and then shut my laptop and pretend like I didn't post about it at all.

Then about a year and a half into working my business, I got cancer. I knew that my business was going to change because my primary focus would be on treatment and healing. In February of 2014, with a four-year-old and not quite four-month-old, I was going to embark on a nine-month journey to eradicate the cancer. At the time of my diagnosis, I had just extended my maternity leave to be home with my son and forfeited my health care benefits until I returned in the fall.

Knowing that my direct sales business was no longer a hobby but a huge part of our income, I decided to change the way I looked at my business and how I talked about my business. No longer would sharing the opportunity be optional. I would take people on the journey of what it was like to battle cancer while raising two young boys and working full-time as a direct seller. I started to share the blessings of the business:
- Being able to give myself time to rest
- Never needing to take time off for my doctor's appointments

- Spending more time with my sons—time that wasn't guaranteed
- Working only when I was able
- Creating a community of women who were able to "sweat for me" when I was too weak to sweat for myself

I was sharing the process of building a direct sales business through the imperfection of life. (Let's be honest, is there really a *perfect time* to build a direct sales business?) I started speaking about the ways the business was changing my mindset toward battling cancer, and I began to challenge others' ways of thinking, especially when it came to success and time.

The year I battled cancer, my income and organization grew astronomically. It wasn't an accident. It was because I took people on a journey and shared unapologetically with contagious energy how the business was changing my life.

I want to make this clear. My success wasn't about cancer; it happened despite the cancer. I had a deeply personal reason for building a business that had so much more to do with making an impact than just making an income.

I leave you with this essential question before we move into the next section. What is the impact you want to make through the opportunity? Long after the income comes, what is the impact you want to make? What is the legacy you are creating?

Section 3: Takeaways and Final Thoughts

Messy action. That's what figuring social media out demands. Messy action. Curiosity and a desire to serve the people who show up for you, well. Don't worry about getting it perfect or having it all figured out. Just take action. The entire purpose of building a following is to lead them back to how you serve. In the coming section, we will discuss The Healthy Pipeline. I want you to know that my biggest goal as the author of this book, as a guide for your direct sales business, and as a woman who has not always gotten it right, is to assure you that the life and longevity of your business depend on what we discuss in Section Four. If you want a rich, fulfilling, and rewarding business that stands the test of time, meet me in Section Four. But before we go there, let's review a couple of the takeaways from Section Three.

Key Takeaways:
- A Staple Story showcases your business, how your life has been impacted by

joining the opportunity, or how you came to see the value of the products you offer (likely a personal testimonial), but most importantly it calls your audience to action.

- How to tell a good story: Define exactly what your customer wants and position yourself as the guide to help them get there!
- Passion+ Knowledge + Profit = Niche
- Your content isn't about you, it's about what you can do for someone else.
- The B.E.S. Practice for direct sales involves writing content that brings brand awareness, engagement, and sales!

Final Thoughts:

I guess I should've given the disclaimer that your content planning isn't always going to go according to plan. When I started writing content as a marketer, there was a lot of neon text and "duck faces" (yes, I am cringing). And friend, I think that's the point. One year from now, I want you to look back at your content with a smile and a cringe because it means that you are evolving. Give yourself permission to craft some content that is less than perfect. If no one likes it, don't get mad, get curious. Remember, our goal is to fall in love with the process of *Direct Sales Done Right!*

Section Four

The Healthy Pipeline: Creating the Ultimate Hype Squad

"Your rewards in life will always be in exact proportion to your contribution in service."

- NAPOLEON HILL

I have no one to invite!" I sensed her frustration as she held up her notebook with a list of about ten names on the page. She'd been a distributor in my organization for about three months and her warm market was just short of dried up. She was in panic mode. There was no one on her list left to invite. She hadn't left any stone unturned. Clearly, it was time to throw in the towel. So, I told her, "Okay! Let's pack it up. Good try. Time to move on!"

Just kidding (I hope you got that joke). Of course, it wasn't time to pack up and call it a day. It was simply time to talk about what I call The Healthy Pipeline.

The Healthy Pipeline is the intentional movement of your followers to customers and team members. The pipeline practice was an unintentionally discovered strategy I created when having my own, "Oh snap! Who do I invite?" moment in business.

The Healthy Pipeline is a consistent, intentional flow of followers, to customers, to loyal customers, to team members, all of which keeps the conversations flowing.

Let me ask you a few questions before I educate you on The Healthy Pipeline:

- Do you want long-term sustainable growth?
- Do you want to feel like there is always a pool of people to invite?
- Do you want to see consistency in your conversations without the inertia effect?
- Do you want a constant state of momentum in your business?

I am guessing you are saying "yes." Or maybe you stood up and yelled, "AB-SO-FREAKIN-LUTELY," followed by a loud, "Whoop whoop!"

Here's what you need to know: I can't make this section fun or sexy. This is the heartbeat of a thriving business. This is what moves you from playing around with direct sales to owning the industry. But this is work. This is nose to the grindstone, tracking your business, having conversations, following up, asking for referrals, setting up Zoom meetings kind of work. Building a pipeline and knowing how to nurture your audience in each section of the pipeline is:

- The secret sauce
- The bread and butter

- The magic potion

It's the mind-blowing, game-changing, holy-cow-it's-actually-working effect. In other words, implement this strategy and you will see your business grow, and then I will gladly proclaim, "See? I told you so!"

There are four areas of the pipeline that we will cover, starting with how to serve your customers and then following with how to move them through the pipeline:

- Followers
- Customers
- Loyal/Repeat Customers
- Team Members

Roll up your sleeves, sister. We're getting to work. Not in a "hustle and slay the day" kind of way, but in a, "Wow, when I apply this it's actually kind of simple and everything makes a lot more sense," kind of way. Are you ready? (Also, I am inserting a preemptive, "I told you so!")

Chapter Ten

I am just going to come out and say what you already know but likely skirt around (Lord knows I do). The only parts of your business you have control over are your actions, reactions, and mindset. You cannot control what those around you do. I know it's easy to dismiss that, but I need you to hear this: Your energy and your empathy can lead people to you, but their decision to join you is entirely up to them, not you. In some ways this should be liberating, right? But why is this one of the biggest struggles for us? Why do we take someone giving up or deciding not to take action so personally?

In 2016, I reached one of the highest ranks in my organization, and yet I was overcome with sadness and a gut-wrenching feeling that maybe I wasn't cut out to lead. In the process of working toward the goal, I watched many in my organization leave for greener pastures (a subject I will cover at length in Section Six) or gracefully bow out, and I remember thinking to myself, "If this is what it takes to be successful, I want no part of it!" What I wish someone had told me then, and what I know to be true now, is this: You cannot force someone into success. You can show them what's possible. You can lead by example. But you cannot own someone else's effort. Let me repeat that: *You cannot own someone else's effort*

There's this quote I think I've heard about a million times in my direct sales business training. I've heard it from countless leaders and motivational speakers. I'm sure even as I write this that your highlighter is dancing over the lines:

SOME WILL.

SOME WON'T.

SO WHAT?

WHO'S NEXT?

I always hated the line, "So what?" Maybe it's the empath in me, but recently I reworked it to read:

SOME WILL.

SOME WON'T.

SOMEONE IS WAITING.

KEEP GOING.

For a reason, for a season, for a lifetime—that's the way I look at the people who've come and gone from my organization, both customers and distributors. People came for a reason, some stayed for a season, and few have stayed for a lifetime. It's my job to serve and support them, wherever they may be, and to let go of what I cannot control.

What's that saying again? Something about, "When you know better, you do better?" Oh yes, that's it. I didn't always get leadership right. But I did learn from it. And one of the greatest lessons that still remains is this: Serve people for a reason, for a season, and some, if you're lucky enough, you can serve for a lifetime. But we can't white-knuckle people into building a direct sales business or continuing to purchase our products; we can only show them what's possible.

There's this quote that is in the margins of my Bible that says, "My hands are open to receive, not tight-fisted to greed." More than once, I tried to white-knuckle my way to business growth. And, spoiler alert, it didn't work. What I learned when I finally started living out my prayer was how to create a Healthy Pipeline, a strategy that educates direct sellers on creating an organic flow of leads from followers into working team members through specific action steps in each section of the pipeline. It's become a strategy I've gone on to teach thousands of women in my organization and in our Direct Sales Done Right Academy. The Healthy Pipeline is your business lifeline. You cannot create a thriving business without a Healthy Pipeline!

During my teen years, my friends and I spent many summer days at a local theme park, Kennywood®. One of the rides that was made for young love was The Old Mill. I am sure what you are picturing in your head is exactly what it was. Before entering the ride, there was an old, rickety water mill that filtered the water which kept the boats moving throughout the ride. The water would go into the mill, spill out, and an endless stream kept right on moving.

The Healthy Pipeline works just like that rickety water mill. To keep every faucet of your business moving, we need to keep moving the water throughout the mill; we need to keep moving people through the pipeline. The Healthy Pipeline for direct sellers consists of four key areas:

- Growing engaged followers
- Creating customers
- Creating loyal customers
- Adding team members to your organization

Just like that mill, if one area stops working, it impacts the entire pipeline.

Here's the good news. You have total control of your pipeline, and once you put systems in place, they begin to work without much effort on your part. This is why we preach systems at Chic Influencer. When you have systems in place, you can take the guesswork out of, "Who do I invite?" I mean, how exciting does it feel to know you don't ever have to run out of people to invite to your business opportunity and your products? I don't know about you, but I am here for it! And here's a bonus: The strategies you will receive from this chapter are no fail and proven, time and time again. This works when you do the work! Are you ready?

In each chapter of this section, we are going to move through The Healthy Pipeline together. We'll focus on how to grow it and then how to move people through it. Stick with me and you are going to begin to see a steady flow of people come into your business so that you can serve them well, build them up, and ultimately turn them into raving fans and team members. Here's how it works ...

Followers

Raise your hand if you've ever caught yourself saying one (or all) of the following:

"I don't have a warm market!"

"There is no one left to invite."

"No one is commenting on my content!"

"I don't know who to invite!"

The list of "why my business isn't growing" seems to go on and on.

Throughout Section Three we spent a lot of time talking about serving through social media. Of course, it's essential to build a following and speak to your ideal customer, but it's more than that. You are creating an online community. At the risk of sounding redundant, can we recap what the word "community" actually means?

Community (n.), def.:

A feeling of fellowship with others, as a result of sharing common attitudes, interests, and goals.

Building your online community gives people a space to engage with one another, not just you! Think of it like this: You are the conductor of a symphonic orchestra. You're leading people through your content, but it's not just about you, it's the way you lead people to take action. You're orchestrating content that serves people who have similar interests, goals, and values. As you're building a community, you're constantly thinking about content that serves the people who are showing up on your platform (remember B.E.S.—brand awareness, engagement, and sales).

Your thoughts at this stage should be, "How can I create a platform of common interests, goals, or values so that people begin to connect to one another and feel like they are a part of something?"

Reminder: Your content isn't about YOU. It's about what you can do for others. People will not and do not care about you; they care about what you can do for them.

In the first part of The Healthy Pipeline, we are focusing on building a community around common interests that help our audience. In other words, we are removing the "look at me content" and focusing on the "look at what can be for you, too" content.

Building an Online Community

In 2014, when my world was flipped upside down with a Stage 4 cancer diagnosis, I was just starting to see my health and wellness network marketing business take off. In a less than ideal turn of events, I had extended my maternity leave thanks to the opportunity (yay!) but I had also forfeited my health care benefits with the school district days prior to learning about my diagnosis (boo!) At the time, I had never seen anyone promote the company who didn't look like they were at the pinnacle of their health. One of my greatest fears was, "Who in the world would want me as a coach when I am going to be sick and bald?"

It turns out that my followers grew well over 20,000 in that year. On top of that, showing up for my community and talking about health as a responsibility was a new take on a saturated wellness market. I started working out, sharing how my workouts were mentally preparing me for the battles ahead—for the chemo that would drain me—and for the constant nagging question of, "What if?" I was open with the community about my diagnosis, and I became bold about how I viewed health and wellness differently than others. I created a phrase that later became a movement: "Every. Sweat. Matters."

Sweat for those who can't. Sweat because you can. Every sweat matters. Thousands started coming to the page, not because I was sweating but because I was negating excuses and giving them a more powerful reason to workout. The movement moved beyond me, and even today, nine years later, I still see tank tops with the phrase and posts that encourage others to sweat for someone else.

How does one create a movement? In one word: passion. Passion is a conviction. It doesn't just encompass what you do and how you do it. It creates an energy that comes only when you are clear on why you do your work.

What's amazing to me is that I was just a catalyst for the movement. I was giving people a reason to come to the platform because my content mattered to them. Forming a community is a powerful tool because it's building relationships for us and through us, even when we can't be present for it. Community builds your business even while you sleep!

How Do You Create A Community?

"But Katy, I don't have a cancer story. I don't know how to create a movement!"

Let me be clear: You don't need a gut-wrenching or awe-inspiring story to create a community. You do, however, have to have commonality with your followers. Throughout Chapter Six we covered some strategies, but a few other ways to cultivate a community are:

- Create engaging content that leads to conversation
- Lead "free groups"
- Engage in conversations

For more information on using social media to grow your community, I highly recommend the Direct Sales Done Right Academy or *The Direct Sales Done Right Planner*. Here are a few additional tips to consider:

1. Focus on serving. Create content by asking yourself those essential questions we covered in Section Three:
   - Is this helpful?
   - Is this hopeful?
   - Is this healing?
2. Give your followers a cue to respond through a call to action. Encourage them to comment or share their thoughts.
3. Send personalized messages. Little acts of kindness never go out of style! Where can you go the extra mile? Did you notice that someone liked your outfit in your content? Even though the post may not have had anything to do with your outfit, send them a message acknowledging that you appreciate their kindness. Did you notice that a follower was encouraging someone in the comments section of your post? Send her a message thanking her for her kindness.
4. Create content that elicits engagement. People naturally want to give advice, so let them! Ask questions! Seek out advice! Ask for opinions! Give people opportunities to respond in the comments to the content you create.

5. Engage within the comments. If you've created calls to action, don't leave the comments unnoticed. Have a conversation with the people who engage with your content. Instead of a generic, "Thanks," see if you can follow up on any comments with another comment, preferably a question. Make it a game. Don't be the ender of the conversation, keep it going!

6. Add value to your content. Remember, the content you create isn't about you, it's about what you can do for someone else.

7. Create a reason for someone to come back. Niche content isn't just about bringing in followers, it's about keeping followers because they feel like a part of something unique. Do you consistently share content that showcases how you serve?

8. Make people feel seen and heard. Remind your followers that you are a community!

Need a few examples of how to interact?

☐ Set a timer to engage with followers for 15-20 minutes per day.

☐ Set a goal to build new connections, daily.

☐ Watch your followers' stories or interact with their polls.

☐ Like their grid content and leave a genuine comment that applies to what they have posted.

☐ Follow people who are an active part of your public online platform.

☐ Consider creating an Instagram album called "customer prospects" to organize the people you interact with.

☐ Commit to following the strategy, daily!

When you interact with followers, you're warming up your cold market through interactions.

Take note! Be on the lookout for people who are helping you build your community. Who is engaging with you? Who is commenting? Who's viewing your stories and responding to your polls? These are the people we will zoom in on when it comes to building our customer base. But take time to hype them up! Thank them for being a big part of your community.

Chapter Eleven

Customers

Here's how it went down when I met my now-husband. Eighteen years ago, I was at a frat party (am I still correct in assuming this is a no-judgment zone?) I spotted this hockey player wearing his team jacket and backpack filled with Miller Light™ from across the room. Pretty sure that 50 Cent was playing in the background, but that is neither here nor there. Nonetheless, I was smitten. Head over heels infatuated.

I turned to my sorority sister, looked her right in the eyes, and staked my claim. "You see that guy over there? I am going to marry the sh*t out of him." Listen, we established this is a judgment-free zone, right? I understand it wasn't the classiest statement. Not my most charming moment, but an accurate truth in the making.

So, here's what happened next. I made eye contact with him, he fell madly in love with me, and—BOOM—here we are, two kids and about a million hockey games later, happily married. But do you know what got the ball rolling? What gave my husband the courage to talk to me? What led to the first date?

Eye Contact

I like to think of that moment with the song *Crimson and Clover* (if you don't know it, head to Spotify® and you'll get the vibe I am throwing down) in the background, all slow motion, to create an atmosphere of nostalgia (a far cry from 50 Cent's *In Da Club* that was actually playing, but I digress).

My point is this: The easiest way to transition to an invitation to your products and services (especially if you feel like your market is cold) without any awkwardness is to establish eye contact. A like, a comment, a tag, or a conversation about something outside of what you sell are all examples of eye contact. All those things we mentioned in how to build up a loyal following are now coming into play. So, yes, you can completely avoid the spammy, "Hey girl," messages. You are welcome!

Eye contact is a powerful opportunity to start a conversation with someone and let them know how you can potentially help them! So, now it's time to pay attention to the people who are interacting with our content (liking, commenting, or viewing).

We want to create opportunities where we can invite, such as polls in our stories, the question box, and sliders. We also want to make call to action posts each week so that we can invite people to learn more about what we do and the products that we sell. On top of that, we want to share our marketing. Eye contact is taking the initiative to ask. If you're scared to ask, the best advice I can give you is to feel the fear and do it anyway.

One of the people I was scared to ask when I started in direct sales was a woman I went to high school with. She and I were in different friend groups. She was much cooler than me. I mean, her high school squad even had a nickname, ELITE 11. Truth be told, I knew she was into fitness, and she would leave a comment on some of my posts, but I was afraid to reciprocate eye contact.

My high school fears of being rejected were still fiercely present, and I thought her comments (although they seemed nice) were a passive way of making fun of me. Even as I am typing this, I am picturing you shaking your head in agreement and thinking of the women in your own life who you may be scared to ask, who you may assume aren't interested in what you have to offer, or who you don't think would ever do something like this.

I want you to know that I understand your fear. I do. It's real. But hear me out: What would happen if making eye contact, and starting a conversation, changed everything?

If you're wondering how the story ended and if I ever made eye contact, I was fortunate enough that she made eye contact with me. Her curiosity led to a great conversation, which later led to a sale, which turned into a ten-year business partnership. But I know that isn't always the case. I wince thinking of all the missed opportunities and the ones who got away because I never made eye contact. So, any opportunity we have to create eye contact is a win!

Calls to Action

In your content, create calls to action that begin a conversation. A call to action is an open invitation for your followers to interact with you. Examples include:

- Tag a mom who is doing a good job!
- Comment below with (INSERT)
- Head to my stories for more information!
- Share this post with a friend who needs this reminder.

- DM (direct message) me with questions you have regarding (INSERT).
- Drop a heart to learn more!
- Click the link in my bio for more information.
- Comment below with your favorite emoji and I'll send you additional information.

Any time my content receives a like or brings someone to my stories, that means eye contact has been made. It's time to extend the invitation!

How to Begin the Invite Process

Now, before you word vomit all over the other person (and I know it's exciting), we want to ask some questions about:

- What interests them most about (insert offer)?
- What are their current goals (that relate to your offer)?
- What are they currently doing/using?
- What are their biggest challenges with (insert product)?
- What are they looking for?
- What price point are they hoping to stay between?

In the next chapter, we are going to uncover specific ways to overcome objections, but starting with specific questions eliminates a lot of those objections. It's kind of like collecting armor to defend yourself from the dreaded "no." So, it is important for you to be confident and bold with the words you use.

- Reassure them that the product you are sharing is a solution for them.
- Make a personal recommendation based on the information you have about the best options for them, and explain why you made that specific recommendation.
- Ask questions to get a response.

When people sign up with you or purchase from you, they are admitting that you are the guide, leading them in the right direction. Don't take that role lightly. Customers sign up because they believe what you say. They continue to stay around because you've delivered on your promise. Serving them during their initial sign-up and the first stages of experiencing the product is critical, because we don't want to clog the pipeline. In my professional experience, we often throw away the most income potential because we see people as initial sales, not lifetime customers. Can you imagine what your own commissions and income would look like if every customer who purchased from you became a *lifelong* customer? Now that's the power of residual income! Our job is to serve people so well that they want to come back again.

Excellent Customer Service

When it comes to customer service, the Golden Rule is never going to go out of style. In his book, *Know What You're FOR*, Jeff Henderson reminds us of the old adage, "Be kind. For everyone you meet is fighting a hard battle. It's true for you. It's true for me. It's true for every one of your customers." We sometimes forget that on the other end of a transaction is a person who's invested their money in what we have to offer. According to Jeff:

People wouldn't care if 74% of the brands they used disappeared. People surveyed also stated that only 27% of the brands are ones they use to make their life better.[8]

Gulp. I don't know about you, but I don't want to be a part of those percentages, do you? I want to create a memorable experience for my customer that brings them back time and time again and possibly brings them to the opportunity as well.

To serve people well, think about what the customer experience will entail for the first month. Remember too, this can be unique to your offer. It doesn't have to be what the company is doing or what your upline does. It can be created by you, uniquely, for the people you serve.

Considerations for Excellent Customer Service:
- What does it look like when someone signs up with you?
  - Send a welcome message when someone purchases.
  - Create a welcome post in your VIP group and introduce your new customer.
  - Send a personalized note about the products they've purchased.
  - Send a free sample of a product that would be a great complement to their order.
- What is the follow up system?
  - Do you check in with the customer when the product is received?
  - Is there a VIP experience or private group you offer?
    - » Do you offer giveaways?
    - » Do you let this group know first of any new products launching?
    - » Do you provide additional tips and strategies for using the products or complementary content that might enhance their experience using

---

8 Jeff Henderson, *Know What You're FOR*, ebook edition, (Zondervan, 2019).

the products?
- ○ What can they expect when using the product? Is there anything they should expect?
  - » For example, if you sell clothing, is there anything you've personally learned about the best way to wash and preserve the color? If you provide supplements, is there anything that they should be on the lookout for? Expectations? Side effects?
  - » If it's a results-based product, how long will it take to begin experiencing results?
- • How do you handle troubles that arise?
  - ○ Do you handle customer complaints or defer them to the customer service department?
  - ○ Do you follow up with the customer to ensure the appropriate corrections have been made?
  - ○ Do you go the extra mile—possibly with a handwritten note or a product sample?

My mindset towards selling changed when I stopped thinking of "closing the sale" as an actual "closing" and more of a "beginning." Did you notice that we are only halfway through The Healthy Pipeline, yet so many people *stop* fostering relationships when the sale is closed?! I cannot emphasize this enough: this is where most direct sellers *stop*.

But not you. Not this time. You are now well on your way to *Direct Sales Done Right!* This, my friend, is just the start.

When it comes to making a sale, let me ask you an honest question. Whether you are a leader in the industry or brand new to the direct sales space, what excites you more? The first-time sale? Or the comeback customer? To be honest, it wasn't until about six years into my business that I saw the most mind-blowing shift in my residual income. I began to see my first-time customers as more of a trial basis. My job was to serve so well that I moved them out of the trial basis into the loyalty category.

I knew that creating lifelong customers would exponentially increase my income, but I had been so focused on benchmarks created by the company that I never put an emphasis on retaining customers. I was so focused on first-time sales that I didn't view my offers as a unique experience to keep the customer.

So, when I made a conscious effort to serve people well, track my ongoing customers, and strategically serve so that they wanted to come back, my income grew.

First-time sales are cool. Residual income through serving well is mind-blowing.

How do we move our first-time customers to loyal customers? Like the Golden Rule, exceptional customer service is about creating a memorable experience. At the end of the day, people want three things from you:

- They want to be seen.
- They want to feel appreciated.
- They want to know they are heard.

When they have a memorable experience, they are more likely to become loyal/repeat customers. So how do we serve loyal customers? I am so glad you asked!

Loyal/Repeat Customers

I hope that now you see why exceptional customer service matters. When we serve people well and they love our products, and more importantly, when they get a good feeling working with us, we have the potential to continue generating revenue without even thinking about it. How? Loyalty. How do you know if you've gained the loyalty of a customer? Here are a few key clues to be on the lookout for:

1. If you offer auto-ship through your direct sales company, they are set up! They have reordered products monthly or quarterly (based on your auto-ship setup) at least three times.
2. They inquire about other products that would complement their original order.
3. They are interested in the launches of new products that you share in emails or VIP groups.
4. They are sharing your products and services with friends and family.
5. They hype you up on your public profile. Usually, they are the most genuine supporters and are constantly shouting out your products and services in the comments section.

At this point, one of two things may come to mind: "I can think of people who fit that bill," or, "Gosh, I don't know anyone who fits that bill."

The good news is that whether you already have loyal customers or feel you would like to spend more time building loyalty, it's easy to do. But there is a strategy. And listen, if it's not been a strategy you've implemented already, don't get angry about it. Just implement it!

The 3 Rs of Loyalty: Reorders, Referrals, and Recommendations

When you're consciously seeking to gain customer loyalty, ask for the reorder of the product, ask if they know anyone interested in learning more about the products, and provide recommendations for products that complement what they are already using! The 3 Rs are an organic way to continue building your Healthy Pipeline.

Sometimes we get so focused on the sale or our goals that we lose sight of the person. It happens a lot in direct sales, but we are committed to doing *Direct Sales Done Right* here, right? So, when we are doing direct sales the right way, we are confident that we are giving our customers an experience that they want to talk about.

Remember, no matter how many people are in your company or how many people are selling what you do, no one can do it quite like you.

Here are a few questions you can ask yourself in order to reflect on your customer's loyalty:

- What does it look like to work with me?
- What can I offer that sets me apart from others in the industry?
- What feedback have I gotten from customers?
- What is my customer's experience from start to finish?
- Would this customer look forward to reordering from me?
- Do I feel confident asking this customer for a referral?
- Do I look forward to recommending additional products to my current customers that complement what they've purchased from me?

As you reflect on these questions, it might be helpful to return to the Unique Sharing Proposition we discussed in Chapter Eight (if it doesn't ring a bell, take a minute to go back to page 105 and jog your memory. I promise, it's worth it). You may notice that building loyalty through the Unique Sharing Proposition means that loyalty actually starts long before the sale. How you position yourself publicly and how you serve people should be evident.

So, What Builds Loyalty?

Ongoing excellent customer service and loyalty programs build ongoing sales! Yes, at this point, I might be repeating myself, but serving people well lightens your load, increases your income, and builds testimonials that sell for you. Building a pipeline of first-time customers that never transfer to loyal customers will drain your battery, friend. I am telling you: Loyal customers keep you fully charged and in control of your income.

Here are a few of my go-to tips that help me generate more sales income without bringing in more customers:

- Set a quantifiable goal for the number of first-time customers that you would like to see as repeat customers every month. For example, if you had three customers generate $300 in commissions, imagine if they repeated an order or ordered a new product and generated those same commissions the next

month! That's in addition to new customers you bring in!
- Provide high-quality service that makes them want to order again or order additional products from you!
- Think of your customer as a person, not a transaction. What is in their best interest?
- Upshare products that complement the products they already love!
- Give them exclusivity that makes them feel seen and heard! VIP groups are a great place to do this.
- Educate your customers on their investments so they understand why they should continue using the products.
- Be there for the long haul. Troubleshoot when needed!
- Personalize the experience of working with you by going the extra mile. A handwritten note goes a long way!
- Create a referral program. Ask them to share it with others.
- Recognize people who consistently use the product.
- Over deliver and under promise.
- Invite them to the opportunity! (Coming in the next chapter)

And yes, if you are seeing an overlap in suggestions between first-time customers and loyal customers, then *bingo!* You're getting the big picture!

How to Ask for a Testimonial or Case Study

Testimonials create additional transactions. Begin banking testimonials of people who are seeing results or loving the experience of working with you. Be specific with what you are asking them to share! I've found over the years that most people who are happy with a product will happily share! Here are a few ways to ask for a testimonial:
- Create a post in your VIP group asking people to leave a review.
- Send an email to customers who are loving the products.
- Personally message those who have ordered and are loving the product or seeing results.
- Share what you've noticed about the customer since they've started using the product (if it's a results-driven product). Point it out to them and ask if they would mind sharing a testimonial about that specific point.
- JUST ASK!

Here's an example of an easy ask: Lead with a compliment, explain why you are asking for a testimonial, and share how you will be using the testimonial and the benefit of sharing!

Hey, Amanda! Happy Monday. Just dropping in to say hello! I am so proud of you (compliment)! I'm literally blown away by how much the supplements are beginning to work for you. Your side-by-side after just two months was mic-drop-worthy (explain why you are asking). Would you mind me asking for a testimonial that I can share privately with prospects, on my website, or in a post (how you will be using the testimonial) so that people can see a real-time example? Of course, I want to ask permission, but I want to shout your success from the rooftops! Shoot me a message when you have a free minute today!

Asking For a Referral

Using the same formula, asking a product user for a referral is a great way to extend your reach without pressuring customers. In the past, I have created referral programs for customers that allow me to give back to the customer as a thank you for spreading the word! Here's an example of what that might look like.

Hey Amanda! Loved your post in the VIP group about the makeup that you love! Thanks for the tip on how to get the best deals! I've been thinking too about the transformation you shared after two months of using the products. I gotta tell you, it's absolutely incredible! My jaw basically dropped to the floor, my friend. Got me thinking, I am sure people around you are getting curious (if they aren't already asking). I do have a referral program for customers who share this with their friends and family. I'd love to offer you a 25% discount on your next order. Can you think of anyone who would be interested? Shoot me a message when you have a free minute today!

But When Do I Invite the Business Opportunity?

In the next section, we are going to shake off any of the nerves you may be feeling about inviting people to the business opportunity, but before we do, let's talk about when to invite. One of the greatest debates from those in the industry is this: Should I invite my customers to become team members, or should I invite anyone to be team members? My answer is simple: both!

In my experience, inviting team members who have used the products and have already experienced the awesomeness of working with you have an idea of what it would be like to work with you as a team member. But I speak from experience when I share that I was never a customer of my upline before I joined her. I watched what she was doing for months and was drawn to the income opportunity. I bought the products on my own through Craigslist before I ever purchased anything from her. I experienced the products on my own and at the right moment, with the right post, I was ready.

Her consistency and her energy sparked my curiosity over time. But imagine with me for a moment if she had *only* shared her products and not the opportunity? Imagine if I didn't know that the doors of her business were open for me? Imagine if she showed confidence only in the products she sold, not in the business she was building? I likely wouldn't have joined her.

The majority of distributors who joined me in the business started as customers. But many of them joined me specifically for the business opportunity. Publicly, we want to showcase both options, but since we are moving people through The Healthy Pipeline, we want to intentionally set up our loyal customers for success. We want to make sure they know the door is open for them. Don't forget, your loyal customers are likely already hyping you up on social media. They are very likely to see your content about the opportunity if you are sharing it.

Moving on to the next stop in The Healthy Pipeline, let's talk about recruiting team members.

I feel like a disclaimer is necessary here. Not everyone in the direct sales industry wants to build a team. In fact, I believe that the option should remain open for people to build a business the way they want, and if that is focusing on sales, that is absolutely fine!

However, I don't want to skirt around the potential of maximizing your income through the team growth opportunity. When I heard the words, "If you really understood the power of residual income, you'd move a brick wall to get to it," my ears perked up.

Chapter Thirteen

Team Members

I know that direct selling is not for everyone, but it's not up to us to decide that. It's up to us to extend the opportunity. More often than not, the clients I work with shy away from extending the invitation to people for fear of the word "no," or they make assumptions about why it likely won't be a good choice for a potential customer. Moving people into the final section of the pipeline means we have to remove all assumptions about whether this business is *for* someone or *not for* someone. It's actually *not for* us to decide. It's *for* us to invite.

As we move people from a loyal customer base into new team members, we've likely made them feel seen, heard, and understood. If we are working in a results-driven business, they are likely experiencing results with the products, and many times they become quietly, organically curious about your opportunity.

Maximizing Income Through The Business Opportunity

Let me define residual income (what we're willing to move those brick walls for): Earning income passively means you don't have to be present to earn pay. (Please do not confuse this with not having to work.)

Yes, we can build residual income if our company offers auto-ship or home direct. But building a team can exponentially increase your residual income earnings. Here's the deal: At first it's not going to feel like you're moving very fast. I remember feeling like I was slogging through mud, trying to figure out how to focus on my own sales, build my team, and encourage them. I felt I was driving blindfolded on the road to residual income.

Imagine that you are pumping a well, being told that you don't know how long it's going to take to see the water, but you have to keep pumping the well to experience the flow. So, you start pumping, and at first it's pretty easy. Not much pressure, but as you pump, you start to question, "Does this really work? Is there really water? Maybe my well is broken? Perhaps I need to look for another well?" You persist, even though your flowing doubts seem to be taking the place of flowing water. You keep pumping. Your arms are tired and you're exhausted, and then …

what is this? A small drop of water?! You stop pumping, almost confused about what's happening. Is this for real? Is there actually water? You pump again, this time harder, still out of breath, arms burning, and another trickle of water comes. But this time you keep pumping instead of doubting your own eyes, and you pump, you pump, you pump, and then … the flow of water finally begins.

My friend, this is what it feels like to build a team in direct sales. You will put effort and work in, wondering why you aren't further along. After you experience a small win, you may find yourself discouraged that more wins aren't happening fast enough or often enough. But if you keep pumping (working), you will begin to experience a steady flow of opportunity. Your pipeline is creating, *for you*, a steady flow of people whom you can serve.

But here's what I promised to be transparent about right from the beginning. Even as you are holding this book, you have to understand that most people will never experience the flow of water. Most people will stop pumping the well before they ever experience success. And that is one of the reasons why direct sales gets a bad rep. Most will give up before they ever experience the good. It takes a quick Google® search about direct sales to see thousands of negative results:

"It's a pyramid scheme."

"It doesn't work."

"You have to get in early."

"Only a small percentage of people experience success."

 "You spend more money than you make."

So, on top of pumping the well, you are likely going to deal with naysayers and opinionated neighbors, or concerned family members who don't get it and are waiting to say, "I told you so." Many of them have good intentions because, well, many of them know someone who has indeed stopped pumping the well or has had a bad experience with direct sales. But what I need to remind you of is this: Luck, timing, and past experience will not dictate your success in building an organization. Your belief that water will flow from the well and your willingness to *pump* the well and build a pipeline will.

This leaves me asking you four essential questions:

1. Do you know *why* you want to grow a team?
2. Do you accept that it won't be easy?
3. Do you believe that success is possible for you?
4. Are you ready to work?

Here's what we do with those four questions. (Don't be mad. This is why you bought the book, right? To do direct sales the *right* way?) Take time to explore your *honest* answers to the questions. Scratch below the surface and then ask yourself, "Today, am I willing to do what others will not to live a life that others cannot, tomorrow?"

Building a Team is Driven By Your Confidence

When I signed up for my direct sales opportunity, I thought my upline had it all figured out. She carried herself with complete confidence in the business, in the products, and in the way she led others. Of course, I had no idea that behind the scenes, she was bravely figuring it out, failing along the way, and getting back up every single time. Her confidence sold me on the opportunity.

As you invite people to learn more (scripts for this are included in Chapter Eighteen), there are four basic principles that apply to your pitch:

1. "Some will, some won't. Someone is waiting. Keep going!" You can say all the right things and it may be the wrong person. Likewise, you can say all the wrong things and it could be the right person. So, let's be clear: Not everyone is going to join you. Detach yourself from the outcome. Our job is to educate people on what we do, not beg them to do it, too. Remember when I was talking about that perfect cup of coffee? Not everyone is going to like coffee. It's not your job to convince everyone to drink the coffee; it's your job to offer the coffee.

2. Identify your USP (Unique Sharing Proposition). I am not trying to be cheesy with a motivational, "Be you, because everyone else is taken," kind of message, but I am here to tell you that being you is *exactly* what makes people want to be a part of the team you're creating. Remember, I finally said "yes" to direct sales because a bunch of girls were road-tripping across the state!

3. Show empathy and bring on the energy. People don't care about what you've been able to do through your work, they really want to know if they can, too. Leading with empathy and saying, "I've been there. I get what it's like. I know exactly how you feel," are key phrases that reveal you see exactly what someone is going through, and your energy shows them a resolution! Great direct sellers are unapologetically excited (not annoying) about what they do. They want to share what they have to offer because they believe it can make a difference for others.

4. "How dare I not share?" When I found myself getting nervous about putting the opportunity out there, I got out a Post-it® note and wrote the words, "It's selfish of me not to share." It forced me to get *bold* about the invite—perfume-salesman-at-the-mall-kiosk bold (but minus the sleazy sales tactics). Asks can be as simple as:
   - "Have you ever thought about (insert opportunity)?"
   - "I know this would be a great fit for you because (fill in the blank)."
   - "I would be a jerk not to share."

   Ask, boldly. Sure, you might get a no, or one hundred nos, or one million nos, but connect this back to principles one, two, and three. It's selfish not to share.

5. Ask more questions. When it comes to inviting someone to join your team, boldly asking someone to join you matters, but asking them more questions when they question the opportunity is key. Coming in Chapter Sixteen, we are going to be shooting objections down like a five-year-old playing a game of laser tag!

Moving people into this part of The Healthy Pipeline is going to take confidence without assumptions. I created the, "It's selfish of me not to share," Post-it note because I knew how much the opportunity had changed my life, and to withhold that from someone else? How could I? Whether they said yes or no wasn't in my control. But extending an invite—yes, that's on me.

I guarantee right now you have someone in mind who would be amazing at what you do. What's stopping you? Put the book down. Go ask.

Are We There Yet?

So, how long does all this take? You're looking at your pipeline, and maybe you're even thinking of people who fall into each category. Maybe (hopefully) you're taking action and extending the invitation. But if you're anything like me, you're likely wondering, "How long does it take to move people through the pipeline? How long will it take me to build a following, close sales more confidently, and recruit people to my business with ease?" How long it's going to take isn't the right question. The right question is, "Am I willing to stick with it, to go the distance?"

When I achieved my first seven figures in direct sales, I remember watching others in the industry fly past me. They were growing larger organizations, climbing the ranks in the industry faster, and bringing in income like it was just another 5-Figure Friday.

Developing The Healthy Pipeline is much like Driving Toward Daylight. Ultimately, you know that moving people through The Healthy Pipeline will build your business, serve people well in each area, and instill the belief that a resolution is possible for them, too. You likely have a vision of what you want to do with the business (mine was getting the groceries paid for), but you have to remain focused on the action it's going to take to get there.

For me, each small sale was celebrated, and each member I brought into my team initiated a little mini happy dance. Every win meant that I was still on the road. Instead of focusing on the end destination, let's pay attention to the mile markers. Let's celebrate every mile you inch closer to the goal that you are working toward.

So, put your hands on the ten and two positions of the steering wheel and begin driving. Begin building your pipeline, focusing on the small actions of cultivating a community daily, serving your customers well daily, providing excellent and intentional customer service daily, and inviting your loyal customers to the business. Just like you cannot arrive at the beach by skipping to the good part, you cannot arrive at a thriving business without taking small actions. You can either focus on how far you have to go, or you can focus on the mile markers, the small wins, the seemingly insignificant action, that's driving you toward daylight. I am going to focus on those mile markers every single time. How about you?

Section 4: Takeaways and Final Thoughts

Everything in your direct sales business rises and falls through The Healthy Pipeline. When you have people in all areas of your pipeline, there's never a question of "Who do I invite?" When you have a healthy business, people flow from followers of what you do to customers of what you share, to believers in the experience you offer, to wanting to join you in the work that you do.

Key Takeaways:
- Commit to serving people in each area of the pipeline. Serving well leads to sales.
- The Healthy Pipeline consists of fostering relationships with four unique groups of people: followers, customers, loyal/repeat customers, and team members.
- Our goal is to nurture relationships in each area of the pipeline so that people seek out how we serve.
- *Invite* people to the opportunity. If that freaks you out, remind yourself that

it's selfish not to share.
- Keep Driving Toward Daylight by focusing on your efforts and measuring your outcomes. Identify the mile markers worth celebrating along the way.

Final Thoughts:

When I accidentally stumbled into the creation of this pipeline, I didn't really think of it as a strategy. I just knew it was changing the way I worked my business. Instead of wondering who to invite, I knew that my pipeline held the answer. I started to see what areas of the pipeline required more attention and which areas were in good health. More than that, it gave me control of the effort I was putting into my work. As you begin to implement The Healthy Pipeline strategy, you will begin to see which areas require more of your attention and which ones you grow relatively easily. I just can't stress this enough though: You need to make all areas of the pipeline a focus if you want sustainability and organic growth in your business.

If you find yourself really struggling to implement the concepts of The Healthy Pipeline into your business, I got your back! Head on over to The Direct Sales Done Right Academy.

 Scan the QR code to learn more about The Direct Sales Done Right Academy!

Section Five

Let's Not Make This Awkward: Having Conversations That Actually Close

"You have something to sell; you are going to have to ask for the sale."

- KATY URSTA

Shortly after my cancer diagnosis, I made an appointment with my hair stylist, knowing that chemo would likely take my hair. I decided that instead of keeping my long hair and letting the clumps fall out, I would cut it short and deal with the loss in stages, so to speak. I don't know if you're like me, but my relationship with my hair stylist hits differently. Like, she knows things about me that I don't know if my best friend knows, kind of like a mix of a confessional and a gal pal for nights out. So, I'm sitting in the chair, she's chopping away, and the tears are flowing. She catches a glimpse of me in the mirror, puts the shears down, and tells me the greatest, most helpful lie that, to this day, I share with some of my chemo-fighting friends. It's a lie I will forever be grateful for, for two reasons:

1. She gave me a life-changing truth from that lie.
2. She made me laugh.

Let's explore the lie and the purpose of the lie. So, mid-tears, we make eye contact, she puts her shears down, spins the chair, looks right above my eyes, and says, "Honey, come over to the wax station with me. I will make your brows look so good that no one will ever notice you don't have hair."

I laughed so hard, knowing that it was a lie, but also fully aware that the woman who was cutting my hair had undeniably beautiful, eye-catching arches. In fact, her brows were the first thing I noticed. That day she waxed, shaped, tweaked, colored, and brushed until I looked in the mirror with unshakeable confidence that my eyebrows were *fire*. The cut was great, too, of course, but the brows? WOW. That day, she didn't just give me new brows (as well as a nine-year, somewhat unhealthy obsession with my arches), she gave me a new confidence to see a situation from a new perspective. ***She couldn't change the fact that I was likely going to lose my hair, but she could give me a different way of looking at the situation.***

Friend, that is exactly what I am going to give you. I am going to give you a new way of looking at invitations to business. For many, the thought of sending invitations feels invasive or too forward. We often shy away from sending invites altogether, claiming that we will get to them another time. So, we create content hoping that people come to our platform, see how awesome we are, and want to learn more. Unfortunately, it doesn't work like that (especially when you are starting off). We want to create content that feels inviting so that when an invitation goes out, it's welcomed. Imagine what your business would look like if you had the confidence to invite people to your products and opportunity, knowing your followers don't just welcome it, they expect it! Imagine feeling like the content you are creating leads itself to welcoming conversations that actually convert.

In this section, you will see examples of how to create healthy conversations, create effective follow ups, and overcome even the peskiest objections. What you're likely going to find is that the more you have these conversations, the more confident you become. I cannot do the inviting for you, but I can give you the confidence to carry them out with some of the most effective strategies that I've used time and time again!

What We'll Cover:
- How to Not Be Awkward When Inviting
- The Golden Rules of Inviting
- The Irresistible Invite
- Assuming Makes a Success Out of You and Me
- Repeat After Me: "I Am a Ninja at Overcoming Objections!"
- The Elephant in the Room
- Follow Up
- The Winning 5-Step Formula for Overcoming Objections
- Ghosted: Their Silence Isn't Your Fault

Picture this: You're at your first middle school dance. All your girlfriends are in a large circle, jammin' out to Montel Jordan dropping a beat and reminding you that, yes, *This is How We Do It*. Everyone is having a blast, and there's laughter and braces and lots of fresh teen spirit in the air. Then, it happens … Montel Jordan, step aside! It's time to slow it down. Perhaps Boyz II Men, or K-Ci and JoJo, or maybe you're more of a Kelly Clarkson *Moment Like This* kind of person? The circle breaks up and, slowly, couples take the floor as the chaperones circle around you like sharks, ensuring everyone is decent. You spy your crush from across the room. Eye contact. You look down. Your best friend nudges you. Your heart is beating fast. You look up. He's looking at you. You look down and begin your awkward, *slow* saunter closer to him, hoping he meets you halfway.

Then, suddenly, that annoying kid from algebra (the one you always ask for homework from) cuts off your saunter and asks for a dance.

Your crush's eye contact? Gone. He's talking to his friends as if that shared moment never happened. Your life stalls with Homework Harry, dancing awkwardly while you pray for the moment to end.

This may or may not have been based on a true story found in my middle school collection of journal entries, but I find that it is 100% applicable here, my friend.

Let's break it down (minus the Montel Jordan, of course). As a direct seller, you have your circle—"your community" of team members. But eventually, the slow song is going to force you to get awkward, to leave your circle and extend the invite to someone who may be interested or may reject you. You may also find that there are some Homework Harrys—the people who inquire about the opportunity that you never in a million years thought would be remotely interested, so you dismiss the opportunity right in front of you.

For most of us, the ask is going to be awkward. Some of us may avoid it completely, telling ourselves that if someone wanted to know more, they'd ask. But I want to pause on that for a moment. Have you ever thought to yourself how intimidating you might be? Have you ever thought that, as much as you might be struggling to invite, others are completely in awe of what you are creating?

I love using this analogy to talk about the direct sales approach. It normalizes that at first, it might feel awkward, but as you do it more you gain confidence, you learn how to do it in a way that feels good, and you perfect the art of the invite so that people are drawn to you.

No. The process I'm about to teach will not save you from hearing "no," but it will eliminate the emotion you attach to it. As you dig into this section, I want you to promise me that you won't get overwhelmed and slide into the habit of only posting about your products or your opportunity. You have to start conversations even though it may feel awkward. Promise me that you won't take it personally if the first couple of invitations feel weird and don't end in a sale. Just promise me that you will keep working on the art of the invite. Keep an open mind and trust the process. Deal? Alright! Let's do this.

Chapter Fourteen

How Not to Be Awkward

As we've established, building a successful direct sales business isn't easy. Simple? Yes, but it does take hard, consistent action. Invitations and conversations are a huge part of the work you do, but I also know that most people go about it all wrong. I am not in any way trying to throw anyone under the bus, but I do think a huge part of why direct sellers feel like perfume salesmen at the kiosk in the mall is because their delivery is cold and, often, uninvited. A simple way to change that is to make your invitations feel warm and welcoming.

When I started in direct sales, I didn't know much about the business model. I had no experience in the industry other than attending a few home parties. I just loved the products and thought, "Hey, if I love it, most people will love it, too!" So, after I kept getting rejections, I started to wonder, "Is it me? Or is it the products?" The answer was *neither*! It was my approach. I talked too much, gave too many facts, and did a terrible job of actually listening to their responses. I was approaching my potential customers all wrong, assuming they needed to know all the details about the opportunity and the product, when what they really needed to know was:

1. Will this resolve a problem I am experiencing?
2. Do you care enough about me for me to give you my money?
3. Can you prove questions one and two?

Our invitations to others need to address any one of these three points if we want to increase our conversion rate. And here's the thing, my friend: As you begin to have more inviting conversations, you begin to see your confidence grow, and guess what that has an impact on? You got it, your sign-ups and sales!

This is where you're likely wondering, "Where's the script to follow? Just tell me exactly what to say!" I am getting there, but first I have a few ground rules. I know, I know … you're a rule breaker, a go-your-own-way kind of gal, but trust me. These rules are ones you're going to want to stick to. These rules permit you to keep any conversation you're having moving forward and allow you to control the direction of the conversation.

The Golden Rules of Inviting

1. Speak less. Listen more.
2. Ask more questions.
3. Identify the problems, and speak to the solution.
4. Gain permission to ask the hard questions.
5. Marry the output (effort) so that you can divorce yourself from the outcome.
6. Follow up (This is so important that I've even devoted Chapter Seventeen to this topic!)
7. Depersonalize the objection.
8. Don't get mad; get curious.

1. Speak Less. Listen More.

In his best-selling book, *Influence: The Psychology of Persuasion*, Robert Cialdini emphasizes the importance of listening more and talking less:

"Good listeners are perceived as people who care, who are worth caring about, and who are in a position to be persuasive. When we listen, we open ourselves up to the concerns of others, and by doing so, we are more likely to persuade them in the direction we desire. Listening is not only a powerful persuader, but it also allows us to gain information that we wouldn't otherwise have access to. So, if you want to be a great persuader, start by becoming a great listener."[9]

Listening is now becoming a lost art of communication. We've all been in a situation where we've been trying to get a point across, only to have our voice drowned out by another person seeking to be heard. We all know feeling "sold to" doesn't feel good. So, to help people feel good about the invitation, direct the conversation to them, make it about them, and focus on what it can do for them.

2. Ask More Questions

I call this your objections arsenal. Asking your prospect questions about their interest in your products or the opportunity, as well as their current struggles or possible fears, isn't just you being a good listener. It's you building up your arsenal for potential objections.

---

9 Robert Cialdini, *Influence: The Psychology of Persausion*, ebook edition, (Harper Collins, 2007).

Check this out. Imagine you are having a conversation with a prospect who shares that she has failed at direct sales before, her husband is skeptical about the opportunity, and she received little guidance from her upline. You don't just have a list of her problems, you have a list of *why* this is her best solution.

3. Identify the Problem and Speak to the Solution

Ok, now that you have a bank of potential problems that your prospect may have, time to drop that solution tailored to their needs. They don't need facts about how amazing your company is. They don't need a resume. What they want to know is, "Can you provide a solution to the problem I just addressed?" Your job is to speak to the solution.

4. Speaking of Questions, Gain Permission to Ask the Hard Ones

Usually, in a conversation about the products or the opportunity, I find the customer working through their own objections and fears. If I am in front of a prospect, I pay attention to body language and intonation (which are also factors in good listening), but as I am listening to what they are saying, I look for an opportunity to ask an uncomfortable question and ask them permission. Usually asking permission gets the prospect's full attention and positions them to feel as though they are in control of the conversation. But asking permission gives you the opportunity to recap (this time in question format) one of their biggest struggles, head-on.

Uncomfortable questions might sound like this:
- "Are you serious about wanting to make a change, or are you just afraid to hurt my feelings?"
- "Are you going to let that fear that's held you back before hold you back again?"
- "Do you think maybe why you've failed in the past was because you weren't really invested?"

These questions usually elicit an uncomfortable pause or a unique perspective that forces them to respond with emotion, builds trust, and positions you as the guide to support them in reaching their goals.

153

5. Marry the Output (Effort) So That You Can Divorce Yourself From the Outcome

This past season, I had the honor of watching my son's AA hockey team win their division banner—a far cry from the season before, as they had finished last place in their division. Over the past two years, I've watched the coaches lean into this philosophy with the kids to "stay in the blue." It means don't play in the green where it's too easy to play without emotion, and don't go into the red where you're playing too aggressively and making careless mistakes. The concept was drilled into their heads at practice, in games, in locker rooms, in team discussions, and further preached at home by the parents. It's a great concept for hockey players, but I've found myself adapting it to my work as well. Staying in the blue means do the work, get excited about it, but don't take it too seriously. Have fun, learn from your mistakes, grow from the wins, and graciously accept a loss. In direct sales, you are going to be setting some big goals and challenging yourself to reach out to prospects. When you remove emotion from the outcome and focus on your output, you're less likely to get wrapped up in the emotions of the business!

6. Follow Up

I'll cover my formula for the follow up questions I ask later, but I thought it was worth noting that failing to follow up is like throwing cash out the window. According to a 2023 article by Business News Daily, 90% of B2B salespeople give up after four rejections, while 80% of prospects say "no" four times before saying "yes."[10]

I hate thinking about how many sales I missed because I thought I was a bother. I can't even begin to tally up the number of times I sent one invite and then decided they weren't interested, only to see my prospects begin working with another distributor. The fortune, my friend, is in the follow up (hence why I am devoting an *entire* chapter to the topic).

But for now, if you are up for a challenge, go into your messages. Go back to your conversations. Where are you missing a potential to follow up? Trust me, there are definitely one or two, or in my case hundreds, that have fallen through

---

10 Nusair Bawla, "Sales Persistence Pays Off," *Business News Daily,* February 21, 2023, https://www.businessnewsdaily.com/5389-in-sales-persistence-pays-off.html

the cracks or were dismissed as a no. Today, I want you to send this message: "Hey (insert name)! I owe you a big apology. I realized that last month I shared my business opportunity call with you, and I never followed up with you. I'd love to revisit that with you. Do you have a few free minutes this week, perhaps Tuesday, to discuss? Let me know when you get a free minute today."

When she responds, head over to Chapter Seventeen for your next steps!

7. Depersonalize the Objection

We are going to spend a lot of time talking about overcoming objections in Chapter Sixteen, but for now, let's *not* take it personally when someone says, "No." Objections are just an opportunity to share more with your prospect. Where most people go wrong with objections is trying to own them as their fault. You can say all the right things to the wrong person, and all the wrong things to the right person. The objection isn't toward you, instead, it's likely one of three things:

1. Not right now.
2. I need more evidence.
3. This isn't going to resolve the problem I am experiencing.

With the first and the second point, we need to give our prospect more time and continue to provide evidence in our content and follow up with her. You have permission to continue to serve your prospect well and let them know that the door remains ajar. If, however, you look at the third point and note that your product or your opportunity cannot resolve the problem or lead to the desired outcome for your prospect, no worries. *Hakuna Matata*—the problem-free philosophy applies here my friend. Keep on keeping on.

8. Don't Get Mad, Get Curious

This tip alone can completely transform your direct sales experience. What if you looked at every conversation with a deep curiosity to learn more? How would it change your conversations? How would it deepen your connections? There's freedom in knowing that you can't be angry and curious at the same time. Imagine hearing the word "no" and instead of assuming you did something wrong, you started to get curious about how you see the "no" differently. So, when you are sending out invitations, are you remaining curious about:

• Why does it feel like they are ghosting you?
• Why do they ask a ton of questions?

- Why don't they seem to ever click sign up when they say they will?

Curiosity gives you leverage for conversions. So, even if you screwed up royally with your invitations in the past, or you think your ship has sailed, do me a favor: get curious. Ask yourself, "Why?" Ask yourself, "What could I do differently?" Ask yourself, "Could I ask better questions?" Seeing the less-than-polished parts of your approach is an opportunity to learn and grow.

And man alive—here's that saying again—when we know better, we do better. But it's true. Curiosity is step one in doing direct sales right.

One more rule while I am thinking about it … I know you want the invite to be perfect. But remember, you can say all the wrong things to the right person and all the wrong things to the right person. Your job is to focus on your efforts, not the outcome. In other words, the most successful invite is the *sent* invite!

Chapter Fifteen

The Irresistible Invite

There are two key ingredients to an effective invitation formula. To move your conversations forward and close your prospect, you need to authentically showcase two qualities: energy and empathy.

Energy

You are excited about what you have to offer. It is evident that you believe in what you are sharing and that others will benefit from it as well. I gotta be honest with you, this isn't an area that you can fake. You can't pretend to have energy and excitement for your business opportunity or your products. You have to own it. Energy is elevated through belief and confidence, and I know we covered much of that in detail, but it's important to note that when it comes to invites, energy has to be part of it.

If you are dreading the invitation, it's going to come through on the other end, no matter what words you use. Likewise, if you're excited about it, that feeling will be emitted before you even open your mouth.

Empathy

Empathy is about getting on the same level as your prospect, acknowledging their struggle, and understanding their situation by speaking right to the problem they are experiencing or the desires that they have. Empathy, like energy, cannot be faked. It's a sincere desire to understand and to support, often from a place of prior experience. Early on in my business, the expression "Feel, felt, found," was used to encourage our industry to meet the prospect where they were by using phrases like, "Wow. Yes. I get it. That must be really frustrating to feel (fill in the blank). I remember when I felt (fill in the blank with a similar experience), but here is what I have found (speak to how you have overcome the struggle)."

When you combine energy and empathy, you show up for your prospects with confidence and clarity. Think about it. Have you ever gone to a hair stylist, sat down in the chair, and just unloaded your life onto him or her? How did they react? The best stylist meets you where you are with empathy but provides a ton of energy around what they do. When you come to the chair, you're not just getting a haircut; you are getting one-on-one attention, conversation, and confidence through exceptional service. The experience people expect from you is the same. Do you show up with energy about what you do and empathy for the person considering joining you?

Back it Up with Text Evidence

Here's a quick thought. Do you realize that even while you sleep, your social media is working for you (of course, that is if you've applied the social media practices discussed in Section Three)? Back in the day, while working as a reading teacher, I was the fortunate staff member who had the task of teaching students how to write a five-paragraph essay using MLA format (Insert the cringing. I know, I know). What I found myself saying almost daily was, "Back it up with text evidence." You are proving a point, so where's the evidence?

When we are inviting people to learn more about our products and our business opportunity, we are giving them full permission to search for text evidence. In our conversations, when we talk about what the products can do for someone, do we have text evidence on our social media? When we talk about the problems the products can resolve, does our social media showcase those resolutions? Customer testimonials and distributor wins allow you to position yourself as the expert instead of encouraging them to go somewhere else.

One of the most common arguments I get about this topic is, "Katy! I am new, I don't have testimonials. What can I share?" Share what you are learning and how it's working for you. Share the vision of what you are creating and where you and others who join you are going. Share the wins of those you collaborate with within the business! The evidence you share doesn't just slowly put marbles into the jar of your prospect's trust, it also increases the essential "know, like, and trust" factor.

Most importantly, when you've created text evidence, it's always working for you. You've taken the time to consistently show someone what you have to offer on social media, so your conversation through direct message, email, in person, or whatever will reflect exactly what you've been sharing on social media. I also tell people that the worst brand you can build is the "whomp whomp" brand. A "whomp whomp" brand is when you build an incredible presence on social media—the bells, the whistles, the aesthetics, but when you meet people in person you're the exact opposite of what they expect. You know, a "whomp whomp." Your conversations make it obvious that the brand you are building is a true testament to who you say you are and how you serve.

In the next chapter, we are going to take a look at the fine art of overcoming objections. Brace yourself, because, by the end of this book, you are going to be a ninja when it comes to hearing the word, "No." My goal is to have you look forward to no because it means you have an opportunity! Ready, set … let's go!

Assuming Makes a Success Out of You and Me

Just to put my spin on the phrase about assumption, in the sales space: assume the sale or the sign-up! Assuming (when it comes to sales) makes a *success* of you and me! When you've walked someone through the invite process, it's time to ask for a yes. Let's recap what we've accomplished so far with a quick checklist:

- You've led with energy and empathy.
- You've asked her questions about what excites her most about the opportunity or product.
- You've identified why this would be great for her.
- You've identified exactly what she stands to gain from the opportunity or the product.
- You've worked through potential objections based on her unique concerns.

Now, it's time to get her amped up and signed up, assuming that, yes, she is ready.

Transition with confidence. There's a difference between saying, "So, what do you think? Does this sound like something you'd like to do," and, "Let's get you signed up!" If she's still hesitant, ask more questions:

"Do you have a plan B?"

"Walk me through the worst-case scenario."

"I am curious. Are you serious about wanting to (fill in the blank) or are you just afraid to hurt my feelings?"

"Do I have permission to ask you another question?"

Yes, let's assume that sale. Let's assume it's a "yes!" But since I am one of those annoying realists, I want to add a few tools to the arsenal. Let's talk about the objections, shall we?

"Help! I Am Out Of People To Invite!"

Repeat after me: "I will not panic. I did not run out of people to invite." About three months into my business, I lost some steam when it came to who to invite. I hadn't put a lot of emphasis into growing the first part of my Healthy Pipeline (followers) because I was dependent on my warm market. It's a common struggle for many in direct sales. There's a moment of panic that settles in and leaves us to think:

"There's no one left to invite!"

"I've reached out to everyone I know."

"My list is completely bare."

I am pretty confident that most successful direct sellers have run into this problem in their business and lived to tell about it. I've included a couple of strategies to combat these limiting beliefs. We have to remember, we aren't out of people to invite, we have a whole list of people who haven't crossed our minds. First, replace your old, no-good, terrible, rotten thought and adopt a new belief.

Old belief: "I am out of people to invite!"

New belief: "There are thousands of people I can invite, some of whom I already know but haven't thought of!"

Let's find your people:

1. Adopt the tips in Section Four to continue building your pipeline. Pay attention to the community you are creating. Consistently add value and search out opportunities to expand your network.

2. Review your list. Dig deeper into who you know. Perhaps create three columns on a piece of paper labeled "Past, Present, Future." Who can you invite from your past (think high school, college friends, and work acquaintances)? Who do you have in your current circles (colleagues, moms from your kids' sports teams, Bible study)? Who can you invite that you don't know yet but someone can introduce you to (ask your current circles for referrals)? Think of it as a two-part question: 1) Who do you know? 2) Who do they know?

3. Network with others. Make a conscious effort to attend networking events (even if this makes you uncomfortable) with the sole purpose of meeting people! Build connections with others!

4. Be on the lookout for people. If we put our energy into believing there is no one to invite, there's going to be "no one to invite." But if we start looking for opportunities everywhere, we will find them.

5. Be consistent with your social media content. Consistently show up on your platform with the same type of message. Connect with people before you invite them.

6. Serve your customers and audience well so that word of mouth carries. When you serve well, it speaks for you! Serve well even *before* the sale!

Remember though, a list is just a list unless we take the initiative. Take the list, grow the list, and then go take action with the list!

 Scan the QR code to get your free Direct Sales Invitation Guide, and never run out of people to invite again!

Chapter Sixteen

Repeat After Me: "I Am a Ninja at Overcoming Objections!"

I wish I could tell you that when I met my husband, I played hard to get. I always appreciate a good love story where there's a relentless, tenacious pursuit to get that first date or that phone number. If you recall, there is an epic scene in *Top Gun* where Maverick and his wingman, Goose, start serenading a seemingly uninterested flight attendant with "Lost that Loving Feeling." Embarrassed, she tells him to sit down. I speak for all of us romantics when I say we feel the sting when she lets him know that she is actually his flight instructor. Ouch. Of course, I am getting nostalgic because watching other people overcome objections is fun. It's encouraging to root for the underdog and see them come out on top, because, who are we kidding? Don't we all sometimes feel like the underdog?

So, why do we want to curl up in a ball and give up when we hear an objection? What if, instead of taking it personally or seeing ourselves as a failure when we hear a, "No," what if we start looking at it like Maverick? What if we change the way we have our conversation and ask questions so that our prospect can catch that lovin' feeling?! Of course, I have to reiterate the keyword: confidence. Confidence is going to play a key role in our ability to change the outcome. We need Maverick-like confidence to combat the objections.

Oh and, spoiler alert, Maverick's relentless pursuit of course ends up victorious. Yours can, too.

What is a "No," Really?

First, a few common subtexts of what a "no" really means:
- Not right now.
- I need more information
- This cannot resolve the problem I am currently facing.

Notice that not all of these scenarios are in your control, which means your role is to successfully follow up (I have you covered there as well, no worries)! So, for the remainder of this chapter, let's talk about asking the right questions and giving the right information to walk a prospect through their own objections. One more point that will help you in the long haul (even if it doesn't do much for you immediately): I want more than anything for you to build a sustainable business, so begging people or convincing them to sign up or purchase what you have to offer isn't going to make anyone feel good. Instead, we want to focus on serving them a solution. Let's go into any conversation thinking to ourselves, "How can what I do or the products I offer *serve* my prospect?" If you feel like you have to convince people to sign up, it's not serving *them*, it's *self-serving*.

Objections? Come at me, BRUH!

I am going to walk you through a couple of examples of objections, but what I want you to note is that every single example raises an opportunity to ask clarifying questions. The answer to the questions gives you more information. More information is your armor.

*Note, since I don't know your specific direct sales business, I am going to give you a couple of general examples for your products, but most of the examples are going to apply to your business opportunity. If you would like more examples, I encourage you to head over to our Direct Sales Done Right Academy.

 Scan the QR code to learn more about the Direct Sales Done Right Academy!

Below, you will find the most common objections to the business opportunity or direct sales products, followed by a *bold* clarifying question that you can ask, as well as a response you can formulate to the objection. In most cases, the clarifying questions will give you control of the conversation. Most responses to clarifying questions are general enough to craft a response similar to the ones listed below. Please DO NOT copy and paste my responses. They are real-life examples of how I would overcome objections from my personal experience. Use them as a guide!

Hint: You will likely notice that each response follows the formula "feel, felt, found" that we discussed in Chapter Fourteen. See?! It's all coming together!

Objection: "I don't want to commit to a subscription or auto-ship."
Clarifying questions: "Oh! Have you had experience with a subscription before?"
Most common prospect response: "No (or yes). I don't like being charged for

something I don't know if I will need."

Example response: "I understand that a subscription or auto-ship program may not be for everyone! And with that, no worries, you can always cancel/modify at any time. We do have the option for one-time purchases, but I am all for helping people save money. Plus, there are also some amazing perks with a subscription! So, if it helps, would you like me to send you a text reminder when your order is going to renew?"

Objection: "It's too expensive!"

Clarifying questions: "I understand! Is there a budget you are working within?

Most common prospect response: Usually they state a budget range that's a little under what you are promoting.

Example response: "No worries! I completely understand that cost is a concern! But here's what I've found about our products. They are made with high-quality ingredients and are designed to last. Plus, we often offer specials and discounts that can help make the products more affordable. In the long run, our products are a great investment in your health and well-being. If this is not in your budget, I do have a couple of alternatives! Can I take a minute to provide those options?"

Now, check out some of these examples of overcoming business opportunity objections!

Objection: "I don't have enough time."

Clarifying question: "How much time do you think it takes?"

Most common prospect response: "I am not sure! I guess X hours."

Example Response: "I completely understand! When I first started in direct sales I was working full-time as a teacher with a toddler and a stack of dirty dishes in the sink that never seemed to end! But what I quickly learned is that direct sales allows you to build a business in the time you do have. For me, that was usually right after school, before I picked my son up from daycare, and an hour in the evening. What I found was that, because I only had a couple of hours every day, I became really good at managing my time! Does that make sense?"

Objection: "It's too expensive."

Clarifying question: "Is there a price range you would like to stay within?"

Most common prospect response: "Not sure. I guess X."

Response: "I hear you, and the good news is that you don't need a lot of money to get started with direct sales. Many companies offer starter kits or other affordable options to help you get up and running. Plus, as you start to build your business, you'll have the opportunity to earn commissions and bonuses that can help you grow your income. Does that sound like something you are looking for?"

Objection: "I'm not good at sales."
Clarifying question: "What do you mean by that?"
Most common prospect answer: "Not sure. I just don't have a background in sales, and I can't imagine being able to do it like you."
Response: "Oh Lord! I hear you! LOL! I was legit terrible when I started. I had a background in education, so no sales background either. But here's what I've found. Sales don't come naturally to most successful direct sellers. It's more about sharing your experience with others! Plus, we've got incredible trainings to get our distributors started with confidence and support. I swear the skills become more natural over time and so does your confidence! I'd love to show you some of our team members' content that has created sales (even though they too once said they weren't good at sales!) Can I pull up those examples for you?"

Objection: "I've tried direct sales before! It doesn't work."
Clarifying question: "Really? Can you tell me about your experience?"
Most common prospect answer: Answers will vary, but usually the prospect didn't feel fully supported, didn't understand the work required, it wasn't the right time, or didn't align with the company.
Response: "I'm sorry to hear that you've had a negative experience with direct sales in the past. But here's the thing, remember that every company and every opportunity is different. With the right company, the right products, and the right team, you can have a positive experience and achieve your goals and fall in love with the process. Plus, I am legit partial, but our team is unique; we're committed to providing a supportive and positive community where everyone can thrive. Does that sound like the environment you are looking for?"

Objection: "I wouldn't know who to invite!"
Clarifying question: "Would you be open to hearing about the invite process that I've used to support my distributors in getting started?"

Most common prospect response: Usually the prospect gives a reluctant "maybe" or "not right now."

Response: "I completely understand your concerns, and the good news is that you don't have to rely solely on your friends and family to build your business. There are many different ways to reach potential customers and team members, from social media to events and more. Plus, with our training and support, we can help you build a sustainable business that doesn't rely on constantly reaching out to your inner circle. Does that make sense?"

Wow! Do you see how it's all coming together? Let me point out a few key factors from these scenarios ...

1. The most common initial response to a clarifying question is a form of, "I don't know." What does that tell you? It tells you that your prospect is defaulting to "no" not because of what they know but because of what they subconsciously tell themselves. Usually, "I don't know," is more an indicator of, "This could be right, but I have some fears," or, "This is a possibility, but I need more information."

2. In each example, there is a mix of energy and empathy. You feel for the prospect. You get it. Maybe you haven't been there exactly, but you have an experience that validates their own. You are making the prospect feel seen and heard. Plus, it's obvious that you have a solution to their current situation or problem. Your energy is speaking for you!

3. The "feel, felt, found" formula applies to those objections because it forces you to lead with empathy! It gives that additional assurance that you aren't just there for the sale, you're there to serve.

4. This is my favorite. Are you ready for it? While you're sharing your response, remember that you've got all that text evidence on your social media to support what you are sharing in your conversation. BOOM. I KNOW, RIGHT?!

5. I overcame each objection by asking them to take action! No, I didn't always ask for the sale, but asking questions like, "Does that make sense," or, "Do you have a minute for me to walk you through some examples," or, "Is this the type of community you are looking for," all elicit an immediate response and keep the conversation moving!

How much fun are these objections?! I don't know about you, but I geek out about this stuff. I am ready and excited to hear a "no" because, hot diggity dang,

I am armed! In the words of my boys before they start a wrestling match in the family room, "Come at me, bruh!"

1. Ask more questions.
2. Provide empathy and energy.
3. Use "feel, felt, found."
4. Back it up with text evidence.
5. Ask for action!

AIN'T NO STOPPING ME NOW! I'VE GOT MAVERICK-LIKE CONFIDENCE AND I AM READY TO SOAR!!! (I know, cheesy, but I got excited, okay?!)

The Elephant in the Room

Possibly the most common objection when it comes to the direct sales opportunity is ... let's just come right out and say it, shall we?

"Isn't this a pyramid scheme?"

A true story about yours truly: The first time I heard this phrase was from the husband of a woman who was thinking about signing up as a distributor with my team. She had already had amazing results with the products, and it was notable to everyone around her that her confidence had skyrocketed through her experience. Her husband couldn't deny the products worked. He had even thanked me multiple times for helping him "get his wife back." He believed in the products; he did not believe in the business.

So, when he asked me, "Isn't this a pyramid scheme," I responded the only way I knew how.

"What do you mean by that?"

Halt. That question, unbeknownst to me, became one of the most powerful questions for every objection (and if I had to tally them up over my eleven years with the company, that would be in the thousands) I ever came up against in my direct sales business. But at the time, I didn't know what he meant by that. As I said, I went into direct sales to get the groceries paid for. I didn't see it as a career. I didn't even know it was an option.

As he fumbled through a response to my question, I listened intently as he used phrases like, "Get in early," or, "Only the guy on top makes all the money." I responded to his questions saying, "I don't have any experience with any of that. I am creating a team and my team members are creating commissions." (Insert utter confusion on my end.)

That night, I went to Google and searched "pyramid scheme." I will save you the trouble, it's defined as:

Form of investment (illegal in the US and elsewhere) in which each paying participant recruits two further participants, with returns being given to early participants using money contributed by later ones.

I want to emphasize the keyword "illegal." I remember seeing that word and knowing that:

1. I wasn't doing anything illegal, and
2. The man who called it a pyramid scheme had never really Googled "pyramid scheme."

Let me shoot straight. A pyramid scheme is illegal, and friend, I am entirely certain that if you picked up this book titled *Direct Sales Done Right*, you have no desire to participate in illegal business opportunities (*wild* assumption, I know!)

So, how would I handle that response now?

Them: "Isn't this a pyramid scheme?"

Me (clarifying question): "What do you mean by that?"

Them: *fumbling over words, but something to the effect of "only one person makes money" and "getting in early."*

Me: "Oh gosh! That sounds illegal (I recommend some subtle sarcasm/snark, but that's just me). This is most decidedly not that. It is direct sales though, which means you have multiple ways to earn an income. I teach my organization to focus on two areas. One is promoting the products we offer and serving their customers well. The second is building a sales team of distributors who are serving their customers well! You, of course, can earn income not just through your own sales but the success of your organization! Does that make sense?"

Them: <Blank stare>

I've learned over the years that when someone tosses around the words "pyramid scheme," it's just an indicator that they don't have experience with the industry other than hearsay. Remember in the introduction, I shared that (yikes) I did not always get direct sales right, but thankfully I got better over time. I've learned that most people in the industry don't commit for the long haul. They receive objection after objection and find themselves getting bitter instead of better. Instead of getting curious, they get frustrated. So, when people quit, it's easy to assume the model didn't work instead of pausing to ask, "Did I do the right work?"

We've covered quite a few examples, and I am sure you can create a few other

DIRECT SALES DONE RIGHT

examples yourself. As you grow your business, I assure you that you will become a ninja at the art of overcoming objections. It is part of the job! Remember when I said, "You can say all the right things to the wrong person, and all the wrong things to the right person. Some will. Some won't. Someone is waiting. Keep going." I don't say that lightly. Confidence comes in knowing you've done the work in sharing the opportunity or the products, walking through potential objections, and following up. But don't forget to be a ninja in trusting the process. In the next chapter, I am going to walk you through the follow up process I use. Remember, to follow up, you likely have to get an objection, and to get an objection, you're going to have to invite!

Chapter Seventeen

Follow Up

There's this rule in sales called the "Rule of 7" that suggests it takes an average of seven touchpoints or interactions with a prospect before they will purchase your offerings. A marketing study found that 80% of sales require five follow-up calls after the initial meeting, and yet, 44% of salespeople give up after one follow-up.[11]

It's important to have a well-planned and strategic follow-up process that includes multiple touchpoints, personalized messaging, and a clear call to action. Now, I am going to walk you through this process, but before I do, let's do some math, shall we? Let's say that last month you reached out to fifty new prospects. Of those fifty, you never heard back from thirty-two of them, you heard "no" from twelve of them, and you made a sale from six of them.

Right, now do the math. What commissions did you receive from the six sales? Perhaps we say $300 from six sales. So, how much money did you make in the next month?

Okay, okay, it's kind of a trick question. Math was never my forte but creating an opportunity to make an income is, so hear me out. Of the forty-four people who did not purchase last month, you now have a list of forty-four prospects. My question is, do you see your follow-ups as an opportunity? Or do you assume that a, "no," is a, "No," is a, "NO?" Do you assume that "no" is *the* answer? If you do, are you also good with throwing dollar bills out on the highway just because you're inconvenienced by them? I didn't think so.

Math aside, I want to talk about one of the sweetest-talking, never-take-no-for-an-answer salespeople I've ever met—my son, Dom. In the words of my husband, he can take your last dollar and write you an IOU. He's been following up on anything and everything he's wanted with no shame, just certainty. And you know what? I love it. I love his confidence in knowing that, "No," doesn't have to

---

11 "149 Eye-Opening Sales Statistics to Consider in 2023 (By Category)," *Spotio,* January 20, 2023, https://spotio.com/blog/sales-statistics/

mean, "NO." I love that he is resourceful. I love that he's taught himself the art of overcoming objections just by paying attention to us. As naturally as it comes to him, it can come naturally to you, too.

Kind of Rude Not to Share, but Whatever

At the risk of sounding like Oprah sharing her favorite things, everybody deserves to be invited to what you have to offer.

When I first started in direct sales, I made some pretty bold assumptions about my prospects, most of which were that they would reach out to me if they wanted to know more about my products or my business. I dismissed the idea that people were quietly watching, curiously seeking, but too nervous to ask. I was never outwardly asked to be part of the direct sales opportunity. I was pretty forward about wanting to know more once I had seen enough of my upline sharing successes and wins. Because I took the initiative, signed up, and immediately built my team and sold the product, I assumed that most people were designed like me. If they were curious, they would ask. If they wanted to build a business, they would.

One of my first distributors, a woman who, like me, was forward enough to ask about the opportunity, was a woman I dismissed at first. I assumed that she was making fun of me and my business. I didn't know at the time that she had just moved to Florida, was single, and was looking to take care of herself and connect with a community of others who were interested in fitness. To this day, Kirsten has built a successful organization as well as a powerful online and local community of women who support each other's fitness goals.

In this case, it worked out. I was wrong in my assumption, and over eleven years Kirsten and I have built a strong professional relationship and friendship. But my assumptions about people, more often than not, caused me to miss opportunities, fail at following up, and ultimately dismiss potential prospects based on my prejudgements. I know this seems bold, but the truth of the matter is, if you love what you do and the door is open to others, it's selfish not to share.

Here are some of the assumptions that caused me to miss out on invitation and follow-up opportunities:
- It's too hard for people to get started.
- Most people will quit.
- I don't want this to ruin our relationship.
- I don't think her husband would support that.

- I don't know how to get her started.
- Others have quit. I think she will, too.
- She likely is too busy.
- No response is the response.
- She probably thinks it's a pyramid scheme.
- She doesn't have any interest in (insert product).
- I never heard back from her, so she must not be interested.
- She said "no" to me last month.
- She doesn't use social media.
- I don't want to inconvenience her.
- It looks like she has a great career already.
- She loves the products and gives referrals.

I am sure that I could create a list of other assumptions, but here's the bottom line: Assuming things about people makes an a** out of you and me. It might be a good time to ask yourself when you look at your pipeline, who are you making assumptions about? Who are you dismissing from the benefits you have to offer? Who are you excluding because of the story you've published in your mind about what's best for the person on the other side of the screen?

It's time to put assumptions aside and get to work on following up with potential prospects and team members. I've created a few lists to begin brainstorming follow-up opportunities. Your job is to start placing names on each list. We're looking for opportunities in the overlooked!

Your Customer List

You may be wondering why I added your Customer List to the assumption list. Well, because sometimes we assume our customers aren't open to the opportunity. In Section Four, we discussed The Healthy Pipeline. When you serve your customers well, you can continue to share new products or additional products you believe they'd love in addition to what they originally ordered. However, don't forget these customers may also be your prospects for the opportunity or provide you referrals for others who would love to learn more about what you do or what you sell. After all, when they are served well, aren't they more likely to want to share?

Your "Not Right Now" List

When you get an objection about timing, these are usually the first prospects that I know should be followed up with. Any customer who told you "not right now"—follow up!

Your Ghost List

The list of prospects who left you high and dry, wondering if you said something that offended them? Wondering what caused them to go into the witness protection program? Wondering if maybe you said too much or were too excited? No worries. Follow up! What's the worst that could happen? They don't respond ... AGAIN?!

Your "That's a HARD NO" List

I find this list to be my personal favorite and also my smallest list. Why? Because most people don't give a hard "no" (usually because these are the people we don't want to ask; see the "I Made an Assumption" list below). But I've found the people who say "no" the loudest are often the ones who are quietly looking for proof.

Your "I Made an Assumption" List

This is the list of people who never got an invitation because ... well ... you made an assumption. Let's change that! Who do you want to invite that, for one reason or another, fear has stopped you from inviting?

Now that you have your lists (and I am making a bold assumption that there are a few names on each list), let's get to work! How do you feel about your lists?

Next, I'm going to review my 5-Step Formula for Overcoming Objections. Full disclosure, I do believe that this formula is best used during spoken conversations. Although that isn't always possible, you can still use the formula in written communication too.

Chapter Eighteen

The Winning 5-Step Formula for Overcoming Objections

CC I don't want to come off as desperate." It's one of the biggest arguments I get when it comes to the follow-up, but here's the problem with that statement. You're making it about you. You're making it about how you will be perceived instead of what someone stands to gain.

This is where we have to reframe our narrative from, "I don't want to come off as desperate," to, "They are looking forward to hearing back from me."

Don't get me wrong, I can take a hint. I mean, I can open my seventh-grade journal and see for a fact that, based on all the evidence, my first boyfriend clearly didn't want to be with me. It most decidedly was not going to be Katy + Kevin = LOVE 4EVER. He laid down clues pretty obviously that my feelings were not reciprocated. Sometimes, it's okay to take the hint. But that doesn't mean you don't flaunt what your Mama gave you. Their decision to not take you up on the products or the opportunity means you still share boldly what you have to offer. (C'mon, anyone who has ever been through any type of breakup knows that you make a serious effort to look *dang* good the next day. Am I right?!)

But coming off as desperate and respectfully following up are not the same thing. Below is a list of subtle hints that your prospect isn't that into you.

The Subtle Hint Cheat Sheet (controversial opinions ahead …)

- They've shared they're not interested and will reach back out to you if they decide otherwise.
- They've unsubscribed from your email list.
- They've asked you not to reach back out.
- They've unfollowed or blocked you.
- They ghost you over and over and over again.
- They are working with another distributor.

In these cases, it's okay to take the hint. But in most cases, assumptions aside, our follow-ups are a simple way to increase our sales and our sign-ups.

Let me walk you through a scenario I ran into often in my early career. I was a distributor with a wellness direct sales company, and I supported my customers through online "challenge groups." I used the products and the workouts to help my customers get results.

In most cases, my follow-ups followed this formula:

1. Restate the problem your product or opportunity can resolve for them.
2. Explain why the product or the opportunity is a solution for them.
3. Review their concerns, fears, or objections. (This indicates that you recall the conversation and can give them a clear resolution to the problem you can solve.)
4. Share the potential regrets of not purchasing or signing up, and share the potential wins of signing up.
5. Give them a time-sensitive call to action.

Below is an example of what a follow-up may have looked like for my ideal customer:

1. First, I would restate the problem. In my business, this was often time or money. *"In your DM (direct message) to me this past week, you mentioned to me that you were struggling with finding the time to work out."*
2. Then, I would explain why the product would be a solution for them. *"I know that my private virtual accountability groups, along with a fitness routine and a clear meal plan, will help you solve that problem."*
3. In these first two steps, I identified the problem that my prospect had and restated that the solution is what I had to offer. I needed to help them bridge the gap that got them closest to a solution. Next, I reviewed the concerns to the objections originally discussed with clear bullet points. *"When you mentioned that it's a struggle finding time to meal plan and to workout, I realized that. I can help you with that. Each week, you will be given a meal plan, and the workouts are designed to be followed daily. I will make sure to help you find the right workout, keeping in mind that you don't have a lot of time. So, you'll be able to do it in that window of time you mentioned to me. And because I find that accountability is the glue to make it stick, you will have daily access to me for any struggles that you might be facing!"*
4. Then, I pieced it all together by sharing the negative and positive stakes. What did the customer stand to lose by not investing in the product, and what did the customer stand to gain by investing in the product? *"I don't want you to keep circling the mountain trying to figure out how to lose the weight and being stuck exactly where you are now. I want you to have a clear solution that gives you guaranteed results, as long as you follow the plan."*

5. Then, I put my stamp on it with a clear and timely call to action. *"I would like to send you the link to sign up today and reserve your spot. Will you have time before 5 pm to get set up? (Give them something to accept or to reject.)"*

Clarity closes sales. People are more likely to say "yes" when you are clear, concise, and confident.

Here's what you need to do next. Use your Assumption Lists as your Follow-up List. Reopen the conversations that were closed. "What if I can't recall the original conversation?" The formula above works well with conversations that are fresh in your mind. I hate to admit this, but I often missed out on following up because I couldn't remember the original conversation. But that's a simple fix. Here are a few conversation re-starters that will help you get things going again. As always, copying and pasting is ill-advised. Personalize this for your ideal customer!

"AHHHH! [Name], I am so sorry! I owe you an apology. I know [last month] we briefly talked about [the opportunity, the product] and I forgot to shoot you an email about it! When you get a second, could you let me know if you're still interested?"

"Hey [name]. I am not trying to come off as totally random, but I was at my son's swim lessons when it occurred to me that you mentioned you taught swim classes last summer for supplemental income while you were off in the summer. I couldn't help but wonder if you wanted to circle back to the conversation we had about the opportunity now that summer is approaching again. Can you shoot me a message when you get a minute?"

"Hey [name]! Just circling back to our conversation about signing up as an ambassador. I know you're a teacher and I wasn't sure if you saw my Instagram stories where I shared that our team member, Jenny (a teacher too), just reached a milestone in her business as well as the rewards trip next year to Punta Cana. I could see you doing the same and know that it's possible for you too! I'd love to set up a time to chat. What's your schedule like this afternoon?"

"Hey [name]! I appreciate every referral you provide. I cannot thank you enough for spreading the word, but I gotta be honest with you. I feel like I am robbing you of an opportunity. Every referral you provide is from people who already know, like, and

trust you. I'm gonna be BOLD: You need to be doing this alongside me. Let's set up a time to talk about what this can look like for you! What's your day like tomorrow?"

Ghosted: Their Silence Isn't Your Fault

Although things didn't work out with my middle school crush, Kevin, I did meet my now-husband, Mike, years later in college. Back in those days, when texting was a pay-per-word process, I often felt my text messages went unanswered. I remember not being sure of the vibe he was throwing down. I thought he liked me, but maybe he didn't. I thought there was a spark, but he was sometimes kind of cold. Talk about mixed signals! When I finally confronted him about being so unresponsive to my text messages, he informed me that his mom asked him to stop sending texts because it was costing her money! Then it all made sense; he wasn't ghosting me. He just didn't want to have to explain to his mom why the phone bill was astronomical.

I built up quite a story in my mind about why Mike was terrible with communication, which wasn't even true. And for you, the story you're telling yourself about why someone may be ghosting you likely isn't true either.

A mentor once told me, "Nobody will ever be thinking about your business the same way you think about your business." On top of that, our attention spans have dwindled to less than that of a goldfish (in case you're wondering, that's about six seconds). So, it's no wonder why people may not be getting back to you.

Maybe that mom you reached out to read your message and then got side-tracked with putting her son down for a nap and folding the laundry. Maybe that colleague you mentioned had the opportunity to think about it but then got buried in one-hundred seventh-grade research papers they needed to grade (not speaking from personal experience or anything). Maybe your college friend was stuck at a red light, read your message, and forgot all about it. Maybe your email was sent, read briefly, and then buried underneath about one hundred other emails. Maybe you started a conversation with that follower, but she was preparing to go on a long weekend away with her husband, so it wasn't on her mind.

Do you get what I am throwing down? Nobody is thinking about your business as much as you're thinking about your business. Instead of seeing it as someone ghosting you, just open the conversation back up.

When I am circling back to a conversation, I keep it light. In messenger, I usually drop a GIF waving hello. If it's an email I might even start with the subject heading, "HIIIII, me again! Did you miss me?" The point is, put your flair into the follow-up, keep it light, and just assume (yes, in this case, I urge you to assume) that people can't wait to hear from you.

A Word On Mindset

I know I've made it clear: objections are a good thing. But if we only speak of the objections we receive from others, we are negating the sometimes blatantly obvious objections we give ourselves. Yes, we are going to get objections in the business, it's part of the gig. But I would be failing you if I didn't talk about the objections we *tell ourselves* about the most common customer objections that keep us from moving our business in the right direction.

*Disclaimer: I'm about to lay down five tough truths. This might make you a little uncomfortable. But hey, as your direct sales coach, sometimes I have to give the tough love. Here goes...

1. If you say you don't have time, you're really saying it's not a priority. You have time to send invites.

2. The habits you create start first with what you think of yourself. If you don't think you are worthy of success or capable of success, you will battle hard (and likely lose) to create the habits needed for success. Consistent action is the habit you need to create for success. There isn't a workaround.

3. If you say that you're afraid to fail, then you better get comfortable with mediocrity.

4. Anything worth doing takes *work*. It takes time, patience, dedication, and belief. Unfortunately, society has taught us that we *deserve* instant gratification. We don't. We need to work. Quick fixes are just a temporary band-aid, *not* a solution.

5. You either want to change or you don't. Simple as that. The rest is all the lies you are telling yourself about *why* you shouldn't change or *why* you can't change.

Do you notice a pattern with these objections? Did any one of them hit you? **Here's the pattern: they all start with what you think of yourself.** They all start with what you think of yourself and the story you are telling yourself, day in and day out. If the story you are telling yourself isn't working in the narrative you want to create, get a new story. In Section One, I shared that my mindset as a direct seller shifted as I spent more time reading personal development, focusing on my journey as a Christian, and beginning to take note of my energy and the people I

DIRECT SALES DONE RIGHT

was surrounding myself with. But just as effort in business action is necessary, so is a consistent effort in personal growth. What you think of yourself impacts the work that you do!

Section 5: Takeaways and Final Thoughts

Throughout the refining process of this book, I found myself wondering, "Am I being too bold?" I would write out a sentence and then delete it, thinking someone might not like it or approve of it. But my editor pushed back (more than once), reminding me that kindness isn't always well-received, but if it's honest, it's the kindest thing you can do. Friend, if we were sipping coffee across from one another I would give you the most honest tip when it comes to inviting, so come close: If you do not share something that has blessed your life and could potentially bless someone else, you are being utterly selfish. It is selfish of you not to share what has blessed you.

Key Takeaways:
- There are eight golden rules of inviting, but the most important and successful invite is the sent invite.
- Energy and empathy are the glue to make the invitation stick.
- Objections are opportunities. Enjoy them!
- Your follow-ups are the key to not leaving money on the table.
- Use the Winning 5-Step Follow-Up Formula to close the deal!

Final Thoughts:
After a section like this one, I feel like a gold star or certificate of completion is in order! Instead, I will say this: LOOK AT HOW FAR YOU'VE COME! Seriously, can we take a minute to talk about everything you've just learned over the past few chapters? I don't know about you, but I feel like a quick celebration is in order, so here it is...

"You've got this!"

"WOW! Look at you go!"

"Drop the mic, because you are doing the dang thing!"

What you have in your hands right now is *everything* you need to build the foundation of your direct sales business. At the risk of sounding like a broken record, direct sales is not easy, but it *is* simple. The most difficult part is believing that you are capable of creating a thriving business and carrying on, even when it gets hard.

This brings me to the next section of the book. This is kind of awkward, but here's the deal. I hope you don't need to read Section Six. I hope you can close these pages right now, armed with everything you need—maybe a stack of Post-it notes and a well-loved, over-highlighted book—ready to take on the world. I mentioned earlier that the only way to write this book was with complete transparency. And *gulp* the next section is like seventh-grader-waiting-for-my-crush-to-make-a-move awkward. There's this part of direct sales that, underneath the highlight reels that the top distributors can so often and flawlessly share, is the truth about when it gets hard.

Section Six: Break In Case of Emergency

Read, if and only if, things go pear-shaped, or all kinds of cattywampus, or the other shoe drops.

Read, if and only if, fit hits the shan, manure meets your shoe, and everything that could go wrong, does.

Read, if and only if, you're at the breaking point … because you are about to have a breakthrough!

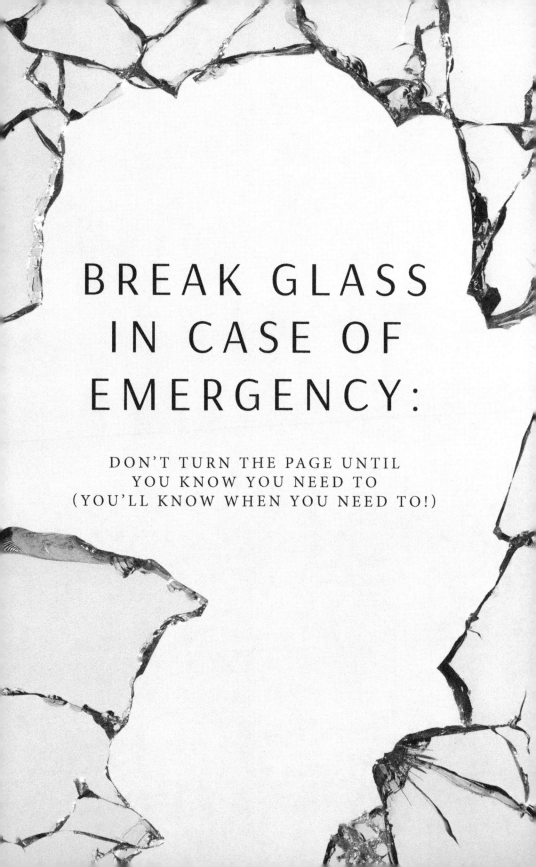

BREAK GLASS IN CASE OF EMERGENCY:

DON'T TURN THE PAGE UNTIL
YOU KNOW YOU NEED TO
(YOU'LL KNOW WHEN YOU NEED TO!)

Section Six

The Healthy CEO:
Break In Case of Emergency

(The section that I hope you never have to read,
but it's here when you need it.)

"For what shall it profit a man, if he shall gain the whole world, and lose his own soul?"

(MARK 8:36), THE BIBLE (KJV)

“ I've been dreading this section." I shared with my editor my fears about writing this section of the book, asking if I should consider leaving it out. Asking her if there was a way to tell this part of the story in a more surface-level way, but she knew, and I knew, there wasn't.

I cannot skirt around the unpolished parts of direct sales. For some, reading this section may be nothing more than a highlighted sentence here or there. For others, it may be the section they don't even open because it just isn't relevant. And then, for others, this may be the section that changes everything. It's a wild claim, and as the author I've had to get really uncomfortable with writing this section because honesty and transparency can't be negotiated. I don't know how to talk about the experience of building a direct sales business without talking about what I learned the hard way.

I've said it before, when you know better you do better, right? And this section is basically a no-holds-barred rundown of the lessons I learned the hard way.

Each chapter will provide an experience I faced as a direct seller that I wasn't quite equipped to handle. I am grateful for all the blessings that came from direct sales, but I am also grateful for the hardships. I am grateful for the lessons learned along the way, and I am grateful that I stuck with it, even when I felt like it would be better if I didn't.

Deep breaths (telling myself this as much as I am telling you). Let's dive in.

What We'll Cover:
- Qualities of a Healthy CEO
- Conscious Contentment Practices to Eliminate Comparison
- It Takes Two to Tango: Open Communication
- This Isn't Just About Sales
- The Healthy CEO Rock Solid Routine
- The Gratitude Practice
- Defining Sacrifice and Success

Chapter Nineteen

" I didn't survive cancer to kill myself of stress." I sat on the bathroom floor in tears, just about a year into remission from Stage 4 cancer. I remember that day because it was just a few weeks until Christmas; I missed the note about field trip money for Nick, and I think Dom was sick. What I remember most is feeling like everything was just piling up. I felt an insane obligation to always be on. I felt the obligation to be everything to everyone. I felt the obligation to say yes to everything. I felt the obligation to work … harder … more … hustle.

But what I really felt was tired. Something had to give, or I was going to break. And that day, I did. I completely came unglued on the bathroom floor, tears falling in between the cracks of the tile. I didn't know then just how possible it was to create a business on my terms without chasing someone else's goals. I didn't know just how simple it could be to realign and schedule my work around the things that mattered most (instead of the other way around). I didn't know that other women felt the same. I didn't know, because I was too busy running to take a rest. I didn't know, because I was so focused on *achieving* that I missed the importance of *just being*.

In 2021, I decided to share my experience of transitioning from being in a business of "more" to a business of "enough." The long, messy process of surrendering to "enough" couldn't be left unspoken.

In a Healthy CEO training series I created alongside my business partner, Melanie, I described the physical and mental signs of burnout: fragmented thoughts, fatigue, a compromised immune system, over-caffeination, and then, ultimately, reaching the breaking point. What I wish someone would have told me then, that I now teach, is this:

- It's okay to take a break.
- It's okay to take a breath.
- It's okay to step back and remind yourself why you started.

And even within that purposeful pause, you can still do incredible things, friend. It isn't enough to just throw out the words, "Maybe I'm burning out." It's a "must" to have a solution for moving beyond it.

In this chapter, we are going to explore the habits of a Healthy CEO. Rest assured, I am not telling you to give up caffeine or follow any type of fitness routine or specific meal plan. There's a lot more to the health of a CEO than what she eats. We're going to explore her daily habits as well as how she thinks. The questions I ask may feel somewhat invasive, but please know my heart is coming from a place of understanding. It's my deep hope that these strategies help you not only revisit your priorities and your joy but honor them as well.

What Does a Healthy CEO Look Like?

At this point in the book, I am pretty sure you realize that transparency, with me, isn't optional, right? So, when I share that one of the greatest flexes of the direct sales opportunity is freedom, you likely have seen content or created content talking about:

- The freedom to create your own work hours
- The freedom to work where you want
- The freedom to earn as much as you want

And while I can appreciate the ultimate flex of "freedoms," there should always be an asterisk that indicates the obvious disclaimer: Freedom isn't actually free.

At one point or another, on the path to a life of freedom, you will either choose the sacrifices you are making to achieve your goals, or sacrifices will smack you in the face and choose you. They'll be like, "Yo! This freedom thing you're working for—there's a cost. Pay up!"

Truth be told, sacrifice smacked me in the face. I mean, straight-up sucker-punched me back into reality. My sacrifices cost me my overall health and my peace. About three years into the business, with a growing organization and a relentless pursuit to prove myself, I started to experience the following:

- Brain fog and an inability to concentrate on simple tasks
- A need for caffeine late in the afternoon to get me through the day
- Irritability, especially with my kids and my husband
- A lack of creativity
- Mindlessly scrolling through social media
- A lack of energy
- A lack of excitement and passion for the work that I previously loved

On top of that, I was craving sugar and falling back into my old habits of emotional eating. I had put on an additional ten or so pounds, and my eye didn't stop twitching for almost three months.

Maybe right now you relate to some of these symptoms. Although I am not a health expert or a doctor, my own personal experience was that my body was responding to the stress that I was trying so hard to suppress.

There's often this mindset among women in the direct sales industry that you can have it all. It's plastered all over social media. But I want to urge you to consider this: what's the point in having it all if you lose yourself in the process? Because, I say this boldly, as a now-healthy CEO and a Stage 4 cancer survivor: If we don't have our health, what do we actually have? *What's the point in gaining the world if we have to sacrifice our spirit or our health in the process?* Sure, you may hit the goals, achieve the ranks, and earn the mind-blowing income, but if in the process you lose sight of your health, your marriage, and your relationships, do you really have it all? I hope that you underline that. Highlight it or bookmark it, because we have to be aware of the red flags that shroud themselves in this industry. I believe that health is a personal responsibility, and it is often the first sacrifice we unknowingly make in our quest to gain more.

The good news is that we can establish some simple habits to arm ourselves for stressful seasons of the business. We can take responsibility for prioritizing our wellness. When you begin to adopt the systems we've talked about throughout the book, you should see that you are freeing up more time—not to create more work, but to create more space for things like family, sleep, hobbies, and relationships (wild thought, I know. Freedom to do things outside of work? Gasp!)

I realized the toll my work was having on my health, sought counsel, and made some bold changes, changes that today are the cornerstone of my overall life. They've become my daily routine and my unapologetic boundaries. I will review the CEO Rock Solid Routine in Chapter Twenty-One, but before I do that, I want to share my personal definition of a Healthy CEO. These are the qualities I strive to achieve and a great starting point for you to consider your own healthy qualities. These are also the qualities that helped me write the personal success statement I carry into all my work now. Buckle up, buttercup. It's about to get real.

Qualities of a Healthy CEO
- A healthy CEO schedules her joy first—before her work.
- A healthy CEO establishes a morning routine that energizes her for the day ahead.
- A healthy CEO knows what she is marketing and the problem she can resolve.

- A healthy CEO has her priorities in check. She knows that there are things that matter and there are things that *MATTER*.
- A healthy CEO sets boundaries.
- A healthy CEO understands the word, "No," and is unapologetic about using it.
- A healthy CEO makes long-term investments in her health, her wellness, and her business.
- A healthy CEO is aware of her habits and how those habits impact her life.
- A healthy CEO asks herself, "How does this action impact my bottom line as well as my wellness?"
- A healthy CEO knows exactly what short-term sacrifices she is willing to make for long-term gains. She knows the ROI.
- A healthy CEO is confident in the goals she sets because they are on her terms and align with the bigger vision of where she wants to go.
- A healthy CEO is married to the output (effort) and divorced from the outcome.
- A healthy CEO takes ownership of the way her work makes her feel.
- A healthy CEO roots for others to win.
- A healthy CEO is aware of her energy and the way certain goals, people, and decisions either give her energy or deplete her energy.
- A healthy CEO does not modify her personal definition of success according to anyone else's standard.
- A healthy CEO learns from her setbacks and walks others through the lessons she's learned.
- A healthy CEO knows that her health is a personal responsibility.
- A healthy CEO sharpens her skills with the tenacity to keep learning in order to benefit others.
- A healthy CEO doesn't seek out worthiness according to a temporary, fleeting standard.
- A healthy CEO believes life is happening for her.
- A healthy CEO roots herself in gratitude.
- A healthy CEO casts a vision that moves or pulls others to action.
- Now, take a minute to create your own definition(s):
- A healthy CEO: _____
- A healthy CEO: _____
- A healthy CEO: _____

When I defined a Healthy CEO, I naturally started to reflect on my own definition of success. I started to realize that the things I was chasing weren't actually aligned with my definition of success. I saw that success was, to me, becoming a Healthy CEO. It was not about the end destination but the process of becoming.

I wrote out a success statement that, to this day, sits on my desk and reminds me of what I am working toward. Throughout writing this book I've referred back to it often, thinking of you, and the impact that this book may have on you. I've been thinking about how every struggle I've had through the process of building a business has been so that I can put these words in front of you, so you know that you are not alone in the process.

My personal success statement (please feel free to steal):

I am content with what I have, grateful in the pursuit of what I want, and faithful in the belief that it will all work out for the good of many.

Did you notice that my success statement is about pursuit? When I stopped believing that success was about the arrival—the end destination or achievement of the goal—and started seeing success as the daily pursuit of who I believed I was called to be, I became a Healthy CEO. In other words, who you are becoming through the process of pursuing matters far more than the goals you achieve.

Bottom line: A Healthy CEO loves the process of who she is becoming far more than the goals she is achieving.

Write out your success statement here. Consider how you want to feel through the process of creating your business. Focus on how you want to feel, not just what you want to achieve!

Now, using the lines below, write your own personal success statement:

_____

_____

_____

_____

_____

_____

Chapter Twenty

Repeat After Me: "Her Success is *Not* My Failure."

A few years ago, I was asked to speak at a quarterly event held by my company about overcoming comparisons. Over eleven years, I'd built my business in pockets of time, between naptime, and into the wee hours of the morning and late in the evening. I'd spent countless hours reading personal development books and attended a number of seminars, including Tony Robbins' and Dave Ramsey's. So, the day before I was supposed to speak, I called my friend and attempted to gracefully back out. I was feeling less than worthy.

Has that ever happened to you? Have you ever looked at your personal or business journey and thought, "I am doing awesome. I've totally got this," until you see someone else doing it better or faster?

Perhaps it's a good time to explain why I almost backed out of speaking that day. I think that it's important to note, as someone who's spent a lot of time on social media, social perception isn't always social reality.

The morning before I was supposed to speak, I received a private inquiry in response to an Instagram story I shared about the business success of a close friend. She asked, "Katy, can you give me some tips on how you stay friends with someone so successful? It doesn't seem to bother you. I find it hard to be friends with people in the business who are really good at what they do."

It was a hard read and was one of those that kind of skew the lines of social perception and reality. It was one that can really quickly send you into a downward spiral of, "I am unworthy."

Surrounding yourself with successful people is not always easy. Consciously choosing not to compare is a skill. Acknowledging the wins of others while you feel like you are in a period of waiting takes humility. Collecting joy instead of jealousy takes practice and a whole lot of grace. It's human nature to look at the lives of others and believe we want the same or that we deserve the same. But we are not created the same and neither are our callings.

I've found in my own experience that comparison makes contentment a million times harder. And through a lot of grace, prayer, and reflection, I am finding myself gracefully content far more often than I feel burdened by comparison. So,

I thought I'd share a few of my practices to eliminate comparison.

Conscious Contentment Practices to Eliminate Comparison

1. Change Your Metrics

Your metrics can not measure up to someone else's growth plan. The truth is, if we are busy comparing ourselves to someone else's success, we are maximizing their success while diminishing our own. It stalls our progress and confuses our own calling. Feeling contentment in your calling should come with clarity, not confusion.

Think about it. Have you ever found yourself window shopping, looking at all of the displays, and confusing yourself over what you actually really like? You try everything on but nothing seems to fit right. It looks awesome on display but not so much on you. When we see someone else's success, let's remind ourselves that it is uniquely designed for her. ***Her definition of success wouldn't be worn well on you.***

Are you willing to continue working and be open to your own unique calling? Are you willing to acknowledge her success without diminishing your own? I encourage you to admire her success, acknowledge it, and then refocus on your own metrics.

2. Journal Your Joy

Gratitude changes everything. Taking time in the morning or before bed to review blessings reminds us all that we have success. Our blessings count as our success too, you know? Are you more busy counting your shortcomings than your blessings? Go out of your way to collect joy throughout the day. Find joy in the process of building your business without waiting for joy to happen when you've reached your destination. Did you have a good conversation with a potential customer? Did you receive a word of encouragement from a family member? Did you listen to the training and find yourself excited to implement new ideas? All of these little wins add up to big successes! Take note of these wins and document them!

3. Define Your Own Success

I know I've mentioned this again and again: As a direct seller, you will be bombarded with messages of success, but have you taken the time to write your own? If you haven't already, now is a good time to refer back to page 189 and write out your own success statement! So many people claim that they want to be successful, but very few people actually define what that looks like. And I don't know if you've grasped this yet, but success to me isn't burnout, hustling, or working an incredible amount of hours. It's not about the cars or the house or the trips. ***Personally, I've found success to be peace.*** I've found success to be undistracted time with my children. I've found success to be making an impact on others with the words that God gives me to write or to speak. It's the confidence I have to share a story, unapologetically, and help other women do the same.

My definition doesn't fit most, because it's uniquely designed for me. Does that make sense? Success is tailor-designed *for you* and *by you*. Sit and ask yourself how you define success. What matters most to you? Then, be okay with that. No. Be excited about that! You owe no one an explanation for the calling. But can I make a small recommendation? Although it's your own calling, accountability matters. Ask someone to remind you what you are working toward, to help you stay focused, and to call you out when you want to give up. We need people in our lives to keep us focused on the things that matter most to us. Iron sharpens iron, my friend.

4. Learn from her Success

I think about the timeliness of my relationships and about the people who played a role for a season. I think about the situations where I could have given more, or done more, but most of all, I find myself thinking about the purpose they played in my life. I don't believe that successful friends are in my life because of coincidence. I often think God says, "You have an opportunity to grow. Be open to that. Learn from her and make peace with the calling I am giving you. Honor your pace. Be still. Be patient. Trust me."

Who are the people that have been placed in your life on purpose? Do you allow their story to be an inspiration for your growth strategy, and do you have a perception that isn't available to others? Do you see the sacrifices behind the story? Are those behind-the-scenes perspectives shifting your own definition of success?

5. Pray for her Success

Every time I have the urge to compare, I replace it with a prayer. And boy did I hit my knees hard in prayer while building a direct sales business. I was surrounded by success and sometimes I found myself exhausted. I know there are likely unicorns out there who don't struggle with comparison, but for the rest of us, becoming self-aware of it is the first step in healing from it.

Prayer, for me, has been how I turned my personal urges to compare into empowerment. In her book, *Battlefield of the Mind*, Joyce Meyer writes, "This [jealousy] is a common trait of the insecure. If we are not secure concerning our own worth and value as a unique individual, we will naturally find ourselves competing with anyone who appears to be successful and doing well."[12] Sound familiar? If our worthiness is rooted in exterior wins, we will consistently fall into the trap of comparing ourselves to others.

When you elevate her success, you alleviate your need to compare. How? It's simple. Root for her. Pray for her. Speak well of her. Look for opportunities to recognize her work. And, I promise, it comes back to you in the most beautiful ways possible. When you elevate her success, you alleviate your need to compare.

It Takes Two To Tango: Open Communication

As I have had my head down, writing this specific chapter and revisiting my own experiences in direct sales, I was reminded of how often I was afraid of having hard conversations. As Brené Brown stated on her Instagram account, "Hard conversations are never easy—it's a commitment and a practice to choose courage over comfort." And wow, as a newer leader in direct sales, I was often so focused on my own goals and my own business that I wouldn't take the time to really listen to what was going on around me. If I'd had the tough conversations, I would have seen that some of my closest team members didn't see the opportunity the same way I did. It's kind of like watching my son begin to play hitting hockey. One of the biggest lessons the coaches drill with the kids is to "keep your head up!" Every practice, in games, during the car rides home from the ice, it's always, "Head up, head up, head up." And no matter how many times it's said, someone always takes a hit because, you guessed it, they had their head down!

So, I thought that I would give you this "heads up" as a Healthy CEO. Hard conversations matter. Avoiding tough conversations can absolutely make or break your business. For years, I kept my head down and focused on my goals, never really listening to what my own team was telling me.

I remember a while back feeling really disconnected from my growing team. At the time, we were a few thousand members strong and many of the team members

---

12 Joyce Meyer, *Battlefield of the Mind*, Faith Words edition, (Hatchette Book Group, Inc., 2011).

loved the products and were seeing incredible results. But in terms of sales, it often felt like I was pushing them. Every month ended the same. I would be motivating the troops, focusing on incentives, and getting on calls to remind them, "Yes! You can do this!" But it wasn't until a woman on my team, a friend who had seen incredible personal results, called me out on my monthly "end the month strong" pushes and changed my entire perspective on what it takes to build a business and maintain professional relationships.

Let me paint the picture: I was in GO MODE. I was doing everything and anything to help my team reach their goals and finish the month strong. And every month, I had the same speech rehearsed. I knew exactly what I was going to say, and I knew the strategy we were going to use to help her close her final sales and lock down her end-of-month quota. That is, until I asked, "So, are you ready? We got this, right?!"

There was an unusually long pause. I probed. After all, it was crunch time and I had to get to more calls. "We got this, right, Chris?"

Then she spoke up, "Katy, I can do this, but I want you to know that after this, I am done. I didn't sign up for the business to grow a team or hit quotas. I joined the business because I thought it was going to be fun. This isn't fun."

Hear me on this, my friend: Communication involves at least two people. She was willing to have the hard conversation with me. As a mentor, I made an assumption that those around me were driven to succeed in the same way I was, but for the women I mentored, it was rare that anyone actually spoke up otherwise.

That day, I realized that not everyone was driven by the same goals as me, and not everyone defined success the same way I did. Mostly, I realized that I never took the time to ask.

Success is a personal decision and a personal definition.

While direct sales can offer people an incredible opportunity to produce income as well as build a community, understanding what people *uniquely* want from the direct selling experience changes the way you lead them.

What I realize now, that I didn't understand then, was that my drive and ambition were a turn-off to many people in my organization. They loved the community and the fun, but they didn't have the drive to build a business, leave their careers, or take time away from their kids. And let me be clear, there is nothing, *nothing*, wrong with that. Where it gets sticky is when we don't communicate our goals with the people most impacted by them.

Open communication between team members builds trust, establishes expectations, and creates ongoing support and motivation. It also creates a clear boundary for both parties.

Here are a few tips to be a more effective communicator, whether you are new to direct sales or you're just wanting to make your goals clear to those mentoring you:

1. Let your upline (sponsor) know what you want most from the business.
2. Communicate the type of support you are looking for.
3. If you need additional support or resources, ask!
4. Don't assume that your mentor knows what you need.
5. If your goals have changed, let your mentor know! If she pushes back, consider her perspective. She may be thinking about your business from a different angle.
6. Speak up, especially when you find yourself wanting to speak ill.
7. Stay tuned in. Be a part of team calls and events.
8. Assume your mentor has your best interests at heart. If something feels off, have the hard conversation.
9. Don't wait for your mentor to come to you.

I want nothing more than for you to achieve your goals as a direct seller, but I know that my role is only to paint a picture of possibility, to walk you through the different strokes of the brush (the action). It's your blank canvas!

In other words, no two finished murals will ever be exactly the same. Different strokes for different folks. That means the way you embrace the business will not be the same as your team members (and it's not supposed to be).

Thinking back on Chris' decision to walk away from direct sales reminded me that I, too, struggled to find my own way in the business. I recall being overwhelmed by my upline's rigorous time-blocking and disciplined routines. I didn't feel that I could work the most effectively without a little wiggle room for creative space. I loved and still do love a more relaxed approach to training and onboarding. Plus, when I started, I didn't have the flexibility to work the business full-time, so taking the same approach that she did to the business often felt like fitting into a pair of jeans that were two sizes too small.

We have to paint our own pictures of success in our business. What my sponsor and I learned is that we both had created our own definitions of success and our own visions for the business. As you look at your business, take a step back and ask yourself, "Am I painting my own picture, or am I trying to replicate someone else's artwork?"

This Isn't Just About Sales

If you were to come into my home right now, I'd welcome you with open arms, kick the pile of shoes out of the way, and ask you to excuse the loads of laundry sitting unfolded for the sixth day in a row. At this point, because I feel like we know one another well enough, I'll let you know that I have been meaning to chat with you about something that's been on my mind. I hope I have permission to get bold because I feel like it just needs to be said...

I know you think you aren't far enough along. I know you think that you should maybe have this figured out. I know you feel like you've let people down along the way, and maybe you're holding onto that, wearing shame like yesterday's stretched-out yoga pants. And I just want you to know, woman to woman, friend to friend, that you are doing a great job.

You are enough.

You are worthy.

You are wired to progress, imperfectly.

You are wired to rise, clumsily.

And above all, as a direct seller, know this:

Some people come into your lives for a season, for a reason, or for a lifetime.

One of the greatest gifts I've been blessed with through the direct sales business has been the people who've come into my life. I'd be failing you if I told you that everyone who came into my business loved it and worked with me throughout the eleven years I was scaling, but most did not. I look back at my years in the business, knowing there are about one thousand things I would do differently—meeting the distributors where they were, for one, and not taking it so personally when people decided it wasn't the best business for them. There were seasons when I thought their inability to succeed was a direct reflection of my own shortcomings, but now I can look back with confidence that I did the best I could for who I was at the time. I also made false assumptions about what they defined as success because I assumed our definitions were the same (rookie mistake!)

I can tell you this: No matter where you currently are in your business, whether it's just starting or you've been in it for a while, there will be seasons that feel a little rocky. There will be seasons where you're struggling to meet your quota or achieve that rank. I assure you that you are not alone. Feeling like you are going at it alone in the business is a choice. There are communities (I am partial to the Direct Sales Done Right Community), accountability partnerships and support systems to ensure that you never have to go at it alone.

Listen, friend, you could take all the recruitment courses and invest in building your brand. You could commit to a new onboarding process or sign up for the latest direct sales training. But, at the end of the day, if you don't believe that you can succeed and that your success will bless others, it's a moot point.

Give yourself some credit, okay? Are you a mom? Are you caring for a sick parent? Are you working another job? Are you active in your church? Fundraising? PTA? Singing in the Sunday choice? New to AA? These aren't little things. Your direct sales business, the process of becoming someone who is able to achieve the goals, is going to influence other areas of your life.

I think about experiences in my own life, with my kids and my husband, and how I guide them in a much different way than I likely would have because of direct sales. The years of personal development I've studied come out in conversations when my husband asks for advice about coaching. My sons working through obstacles with friends, in sports, and in school is being influenced by me, a woman who's been pouring herself into becoming a stronger leader for years. How I speak of my faith, how I speak openly about life after cancer, my marriage, my relationships—all of that would be drastically different if the life experience of building a direct sales business didn't happen.

You're not just building a cute, little business. You're Driving Toward Daylight. You're choosing the direction of your life!

Chapter Twenty-One

The Healthy CEO Rock Solid Routine

"Bubble baths are not self-care. Self-care is proactively cultivating a healthy mindset—physically, spiritually, and emotionally."

- KATY URSTA

I guess I admit it. A long time ago, I stumbled into this ridiculous lifetime membership of the "I can sleep when I am dead" club. But the problem is, I no longer adhere to the hidden rules (you know, the fine print that reads "succeed at any cost"). And as your guide on this *Direct Sales Done Right* journey, I want to challenge your thinking a little bit.

Let me be the first to admit that I saw the #girlboss #slaysister #hustlehard influencers, and I bought the lie that my worth had to be earned, so I ran … and I ran … and I ran. But the whole time I was running, I had no idea that there was actually *no finish line*. The whole time I was running, I was gasping for air, desperately trying to keep up with those who seemed to have it all figured out. The whole time I was running, I was leaving behind what mattered most for what mattered in the moment. Sound familiar?

Unpacking the years of the "do more," "sell more," "be more," and "worthy only when," lies that I've bought into has been a long, unfiltered fumble, an unfiltered fumble of:

- fighting for my health
- allowing myself to rest without explanation
- working toward goals that work for me
- believing that I am worthy without all the wins
- setting insanely firm boundaries
- defining success on my terms

So, here I am. I no longer hustle hard or slay the day or 10X at any cost. I work smarter. I work with intention. I no longer believe in showing up at all costs when my mind, body, and spirit scream, "Slow down, sister!" I no longer buy into the belief that my worth is my title, my rank, my income, my appearance, my social media likes, or my sales.

But please don't mistake that as not working hard. I work hard, but I work healthily. As much as I'd love to tell you that no longer buying into that belief has been easy, the truth is, it's work. It's hard work. It's like a spiritual scrub down. And it starts with knowing myself well enough to know:

- I can sleep in.
- I can rest.
- I can set boundaries.

I can do these things and *still* live out my calling, helping other women see their worth, with or without the win. So, before we get into the nitty-gritty details of how, you need to know that you are worthy, *right now, before you feel like you've arrived at your goal.* Let's talk about some of my best daily practices that have allowed me to jog away from the hustle and run toward the intention.

Establish an Iron Clad Morning Routine

Motivation has a shelf life. Ironclad routines do not. One of the first small details I noted about the successful leaders in my company was how they each talked about routines. At first, I remember thinking, "Sure, I brush my teeth." Or, yes, "I empty the dishwasher after work." I had routines, but I wouldn't say the routines I had were improving my life. They were more of a "must do", and the dos got done around the same time every day. Knowing that success was leaving me clues, I couldn't help but notice that many industry leaders specifically talked about their *morning* routines. Many of them spoke of the time they'd spend reading books, journaling, or praying. But I got so stuck on the time it must've taken them to do these things (because I was usually too busy to even eat breakfast) that I didn't think I could do it myself.

Fast forward over ten years later and my morning routine is ironclad, but reaching that point required me to make a decision to do something small each day that "five years from now Katy" would say thank you for. It wasn't and isn't about how much time you can commit. I know women in the industry who spend over three hours on their morning routine and others who spend three minutes! What matters is your willingness to establish a habit.

When I first started in direct sales, I didn't see successful industry leaders working full-time jobs. I only saw women that had over two hours in the morning to devote to their morning routines. So, I knew that if I was going to create a routine, I had to do it with the time I had.

I decided the first thing I would do in the morning was:

1. Journal
2. Read a book that helped me build my business
3. Meditate

I am happy to report that two of those three worked. Meditation was not and still is not my jam. But the routine was a start. I simply committed to getting up thirty minutes earlier in the morning—first for a week, then for another week, and another, and another. Here we are, eleven years later, with a much more in-depth routine. But creating the foundation was the start. It was a foundation that started with, "What will 'five years from now Katy' say thank you for?" I want you to start with that question. What routine, if you added it to your life now, would "five years from now you" say thank you for?

Maybe it's:

• Daily prayer
• Devotional
• Meditation
• Gratitude practice
• Movement
• Writing

Next, ask yourself: How much time are you able and willing to commit to your routine? It's two questions, really. If you want the habit to stick, it's helpful to look at your track record. What hasn't worked for you in the past? Why?

Getting up an hour earlier as a sleep-deprived mom wasn't going to be something I could do and stick to (I had attempted that before and failed), but I did believe that thirty minutes was doable. So I gave it a week, and it stuck. I gave it another week and another, and now it's a habit!

Also, consider *why* you want to create the habit. How does "five years from now you" stand to benefit from this habit? On the other hand, what does "five years from now you" stand to lose if you don't?

Getting up thirty minutes early was doable *because* I wanted to do more than just get by. I wanted more than just crossing my fingers, hoping there was enough in the bank account at the end of the week. That vision drove me when the new routine was still uncomfortable when I was tired in the morning, and I battled the internal narrative that told me that success was out of reach.

The "five years from now version of yourself" wants nothing more than to say, "Thank you!" Visualize her, waiting for you! Visualize the person you know you are becoming through the process.

Give yourself a week. Adjust your routine as needed. Then give it another week, and another, and another. The compound effect of these seemingly insignificant decisions is the one that makes all the difference.

My Current Ironclad Morning Routine

I feel like experts spend a lot of time talking about this topic. There are books and articles and podcasts devoted to it, but in a nutshell, if you want to establish a rock-solid routine, you have to just start and have a strong enough reason for it to stick. In this season of my life, I am a full-time business owner with two boys who are both in school and very active in sports. My morning routine is designed with that in mind: a mom who gets eight hours of sleep a night, who wants to be present with her kids in the morning, and who has the additional time to spend on her routine, unlike when she was working full-time with an infant son and a toddler.

Your life circumstances are going to change, so expect that your morning routine will, too. You will adjust, but remember, the ultimate goal of the ironclad morning routine is to get that, "Thank you," five years from now.

My Current Ironclad Morning Routine
- Wake without an alarm (around 5:30 am)
- Put on my workout clothes
- Drink my pre-workout
- Bible reading. Read a Psalm, Old Testament, and New Testament
- Pray out loud on my knees
- Selected reading (personal development or a devotional)
- *Back Pocket Prayer* Journaling
- Workout
- 3-5 minute cold plunge
- Time with my kids
- Frothed coffee

- Shower and a podcast
- Review my time blocker
- Content creation

 Scan the QR code to learn more about *The Back Pocket Prayer Journal!*

There are a few small points I want to address about routine. I no longer set an alarm because I trained myself to wake up early (this is a benefit of creating a routine that, over time, becomes a habit). Eleven years of a morning routine and honoring rest will do that for you! My morning routine also involves starting the day with my kids. With a background in education, I know that I would've missed the opportunity to be with my kids in the morning if I had stayed in that line of work, so I never overlook the blessing of being the one who gets to start the day with them. That's the time I built into my morning routine.

As you begin to design your morning routine, taking into account the "five years from now thank you," consider these additional questions:
- Does my morning routine put me on the offense or defense for the day?
- Does my morning routine force me to become more self-aware of the areas of my life that I seek to improve?
- Does my morning routine support my personal growth goals—spiritually, physically, and emotionally?
- Does my morning routine set me up for a productive day?
- Does my morning routine bring me closer to my personal "five years from now thank you?"

If the ironclad *morning* routine doesn't work for you, create an ironclad *evening* routine, or even a *midafternoon* routine. Don't get caught up on the time of the routine, get caught up on the reason you are creating it.

Movement

Disclaimer: My experience with direct sales was in the wellness space. So, I have a good amount of knowledge about the benefits of movement and the connection movement has to productivity, as well as the long-term impact on overall health. This isn't a book about fitness and nutrition, but I would be remiss to not share the benefits that taking care of yourself physically can have on your business. Every once in a while, when it comes to health, I say something that others find offensive. What I am about to say may turn you off or cause you to roll your eyes. But for some of you, this subtle shift may change the way you see daily movement. I can't *not* speak about this. So, instead, I'll promise you this: I come from a place of kindness. I speak from my own experiences, not to offend, but to educate. Here we go.

Our health is our *own* responsibility. Period.

Not our doctor's.

Not our insurance provider's.

Not our spouse's.

Not our sponsor's.

Not that influencer's.

Not our personal trainer's.

Not our media outlet's.

Not our therapist's.

Not big pharma's.

Ours.

If we want to change our health, we have to start by looking at our own habits and deciding on our own to make a change. If we want to change our health, we need to make a decision to actually do something about it instead of just talking about it. If we want to change the way we view fitness, we need to look at the imperfection of starting and lean into the progress found in doing. No matter what others tell you, suggest to you, or refer to you—at the end of the day—health is our own responsibility. Be proactive, start when it's imperfect. Start when you're less than ready. Okay. Deep breaths. Let's talk about the start.

It's no secret that some of the work you do and the goals you set can create seasons of stress. But when we aren't aware of the stress these seasons have on our bodies, it can lead to burnout as well as other health issues. A recent study about how exercise increases productivity said this:

"A habit of regular exercise will help keep you mentally sharper throughout your entire life. As you age, your body generates fewer and fewer brain cells (a process called neurogenesis). However, early research suggests that exercise can help prevent this slowdown. In other words, by the time they reach their 50s, 60s, and 70s, people who exercise might have more brain cells than their more sedentary peers — giving them a major advantage in the workplace."[13]

If you're telling yourself that you don't have time for exercise, I encourage you to rethink your perspective. Instead of, "I don't have time to work out," maybe it's, "I don't have time to be sick." I am a firm believer that health is a personal responsibility, and most of us look at movement and exercise with the attitude of, "Great, if I can find time to get to it." But for me, every single sweat matters.

A few benefits of exercise:
- Clears your head
- Sparks creativity
- Provides natural energy
- Helps manage stress
- Boosts your immune system
- Grows your confidence

Ways to incorporate more movement:
- Begin walking in the late afternoon to close out your day
- Take a Pilates class with a friend
- Stream an at-home workout
- Listen to a podcast while cleaning the house

Affirmations to Reframe Your Relationship with the Workout

These are affirmations that I still use which shift my mindset from "I have to" to "I get to" when it comes to health.
- "I am healthy, strong, and in control of my food choices."
- "My health is my responsibility. This is the only body I get, so I choose daily to take good care of it."
- "My feet hit the floor this morning, so I will sweat because I can, and I will sweat to honor those who can't."
- "My body is fighting battles I don't even know about. My body is on my side. So, I will fight *for* it, not against it."

Do you have someone who is willing to call you out? Do you recall in Chapter Five when I talked about accountability and the woman who showed up at the gym day after day because someone was waiting for her? If movement is a new

---

13 Robert C. Pozen, "Exercise Increases Productivity," *Brookings,* October 24, 2012, https://www.brookings.edu/articles/exercise-increases-productivity/

habit you want to form, ask a friend or a loved one for accountability. Get a buddy. Go to the gym together! Provide daily text messages with updates! I believe habits form when they get out of the "should do" zone and fall into the "must do" zone. Accountability moves our habits into that "must-do" zone.

The Gratitude Practice

Fact: You can't be angry and curious at the same time.

There are going to be mornings when you wake up on the wrong side of the bed. Days when you feel like the cards are stacked against you, and moments when you wonder, "Am I really cut out for all of this?" On those days, gratitude becomes your lifeline. In the past, I've described it almost like a chemo drip of joy (pardon the analogy, I just have a bit of experience in the cancer department).

"Every day in your life your immune system destroys a cell that would have become cancer if it lived." I read this stat about cancer and it got me thinking:

Everything we consume…

Everything we ingest…

Everything we breathe…

How we move…

How we think…

… all of it impacts cancer growth. Let that sink in. Does that blow your mind as it does mine? I mean, do you realize that you are a miracle constantly in the making? Our bodies are constantly under attack, and unbeknownst to us, our beautiful bodies fight for us. Incredible isn't it? The more I think about this, the more I think about how it's easy to put cancer in a category that refers only to cells. But really, we all have cancers. Every single one of us battles the cancers of:

Not enough.

Loss.

Fear.

Comparison.

Pain, sadness, grief, burden, worry, anxiety, addiction, paralysis, loneliness…

Did I miss any? I am sure I did. Do you realize every day we carry our cancer in us, with us, and around us; if we aren't careful, our cancers can truly consume us. They consume us until we become someone we don't recognize and all we see is the cancer. Cancer is sneaky, it grows without you knowing; all the signs may be there, but awareness matters.

We can ignore the signs of our cancer or we can embrace the fact that cancer is part of our story. We can battle back. We're naturally magnificent walking miracles. I've learned that cancer stands no chance against hope, joy, and gratitude. *None.* Consume a daily dose. Overdose on gratitude. Take a constant chemo drip of it and those cancers *cannot* win. Cancer *cannot* overcome gratitude.

This morning, I awoke with those cancers—those stresses and worries—instead of gratitude. Yes, it happens to me. More often than I care to admit. But I've found a chemo drip, a cocktail of sorts, that helps me keep negative thoughts at bay. You will notice that my gratitude practice is woven into my spiritual beliefs, but the practice works no matter your personal beliefs.

Here's how I mix my cocktail of gratitude:

Step One

I journal it out. I get out of my head what's swirling around inside and put it into writing. With the words on paper, I create two columns. Column one is in my control. I list out the things that I am worried about and ask, "Katy, is this something you can act on?" Column two is out of my control. I list this column out and say, "Okay, God, do you mind taking this list from me?" I leave it to God and I pray it away.

Step Two

I look at my in-control list and literally ask myself this gut-check question, "What can I do today to commit to the output instead of trying to control the outcome?" When I list out the controllable, I know that, yes, there is action needed on my part, but my faith isn't in how it will end up. I surrender that part. My focus is on the "can-do". Then I simply state, "Thine will be done."

Step Three

I move my body as a way to activate prayer (again, there are benefits to exercise), to work through my worries, and to seek out gratitude through movement. I work out as a simple reminder that He put breath in my lungs so I may walk through His will.

No matter how many times I share my own chemo drip of joy, my gratitude practice, I still get asked:

- "How do I just begin to eliminate my cancers?"
- "How do I just start believing it's possible for me when the people around me don't see it?"
- "How do I just remove myself from toxic relationships? Conditions? People?"
- "How do I just eradicate the things that drain me when I have responsibilities and demands and pressure?"

Those are all good questions. And here's what I think: it's going to take time. Experiencing radical joy starts with a slow dose of joy. It's about starting the day with gratitude. It's about creating a morning routine that you will thank yourself for five years from now. It's about moving because you get to, not because you have to. It's about saying yes to the things that inspire you. It's about enjoying the process of who you are becoming. It's about acknowledging that happiness is found most often through difficulty. It's about understanding that a joyful life is created one day, one decision, one thought, and one small act at a time.

That's how the chemo drip of joy works.

In 2017, a couple of years after battling cancer, I wrote a post that went on to be shared by thousands. As I thought about the words to close out what I believe to be the most important section of this book, I thought about this post and how, even now, it hits me. What a gift it is to take care of our bodies, but also, wow, what a responsibility.

As I leave you with this post, I encourage you to look at your relationship with your health and how you care for it. Do you see it as a responsibility? Do you make it a priority? Sometimes hindsight gives us a clearer perspective on what matters. Cancer, for me, gave me this bold perspective that the greatest gift we have is our health. Because if we lose our health, what do we really have?

Here's the post:

"When I was first diagnosed with cancer, I was recovering from my second C-section, so understandably, my body was transitioning from one trauma only to embrace another.

I was curvy, soft in spots, and just starting to be able to zip my jeans. I was struggling to breathe through workouts, and my lack of appetite was preventing me from producing enough milk.

I was tired; other signs started to surface. I didn't know about the cancer. I just knew I wanted to lose the weight.

My son was four-months-old when I was diagnosed with Stage 4 Hodgkins Lymphoma. In my first month of chemo, I lost five pounds. Then another five. And another.

I was thin. Really thin.

I distinctly remember a morning a few days after treatment, maybe after chemo round four or five, I was watching the clumps of hair fall out, combatting the waves of fatigue, and mustering the strength to make a trip to Target® because I couldn't stand the thought of staying in bed another day.

Sick and weak, jeans sitting low on my waist and a hat hiding my thinning hair, I ventured out. I recognized a woman I'd connected with years before through a college course. She saw my young son and my thin figure, and just as I would've assumed of another new mother, "She's one of those lucky ones who just bounce back!" She said, "Ah Katy ... What's your secret? You look great!! I'd give anything to get my body back as fast as you have!"

She saw my thin. She assumed health. I knew my thin. My thin was trying to kill me.

Walking away, weak and sick, covering the truth in a baseball cap and a baggy hoodie, all I could think was, "Lord, take back thin and give me health." Health, sweet friend, is our greatest gift. Not thin. They aren't the same.

Mama, who is battling the last five or ten or twenty or however many pounds…

Mama, battling the button of your jeans…

Mama, battling the tears that come when you look in the mirror…

… Battle instead for your health.

Battle to take good care of you. Battle to feel good. Battle to recognize what your body does for you. Battle to make peace with your curves and dimples and rolls and stretch marks. Battle to love the woman you see in your reflection.

Because that body is fighting for you. You matter too much to sacrifice your health for the facade of a pre-baby body or a pair of uncooperative jeans. Mama, simply battle for you. Every curve. Every dimple. Every roll. Every stretch mark.

That's your body fighting for you. Because your body is on your side. Don't battle against it. Don't hate it. Acknowledge what a gift it is to have a body that is fighting for you."

Friend, shifting your perspective from "I have to" to "I get to" every single day will radically change your life and your business.

Chapter Twenty-Two

Defining Sacrifice

"I've never met anyone who doesn't want to be successful, but very few people have actually spelled out success for themselves."

- KATY URSTA

You know how there are certain memories that you look back at with such vivid clarity and focus, it's as if you're reliving the moment? Like you walked into it—all five senses alert to your surroundings? I, for sure, have a handful of them. One of them was the time my kindergarten teacher, Mrs. Bakalarski, pulled me aside when I had tears in my eyes because I learned that I would be reading with the "turtles" group (yes, back in those days we had the "turtles" and the "hares" for reading groups). I can also distinctly remember the moment I received the call that I had cancer and fell to my knees in the workout room. And there are those joyful moments, like seeing my husband on our wedding day and the birth of my sons. But it always fascinated me that I could look back at seemingly insignificant moments with utter clarity knowing that, for whatever reason, I was called to remember it.

One particular, seemingly insignificant moment in my direct sales business brings back that clarity. About four years into my business, I had established quite a bit of credibility and had grown my organization to a couple of thousand distributors, both working and receiving the discount. At that time, I was working the business full-time and had created a significant income for our family. It, of course, had come at a price. My health, my peace of mind, and my time with my family suffered. All of which I talked through, and with the help of a wonderful therapist, I found myself reconstructing my relationship with work. I found myself taking more time away from work and being more present with my family. On one particular occasion (it was late September, a detail I remember because the air was a little cooler and it was getting darker earlier), I picked up the phone while my husband and two sons were all in the kitchen. I am pretty sure the TV was playing *Teenage Mutant Ninja Turtles®* in the background because the boys were running around with capes, punching and kicking, and pretending to be little ninja turtles. Mike, my husband, was joining in the banter and singing along to the theme song. It was a good night.

So, I picked up the call, and my corporate mentor was on the line. He'd called to share my updated team numbers, letting me know that I was only "this far" from achieving a milestone that would lock me into a rank or title, or something (I don't remember all the details, aside from the fact that I was close). So, I listened and ran through some ideas in my head, began to crunch some numbers of my own, and thought through a list of follow-ups and invitations I could send. As he was walking through the numbers and the incentive on the other end, I remember him saying, "If you just work a little harder…" That's all it took. Those seven little words weren't overlooked by me. You see, working a little harder, at that moment, wasn't an option.

I was already working hard. And there I was, in my kitchen with my sons and my husband, cooking dinner—beautiful, messy chaos all around me—and I thought to myself, "I already have everything I want."

Do not tell your upline what I am going to share. If you do, I will deny it. Then again, I do realize you can give her the book and … geez, eek … okay. I suppose I am going to finally tell you the secret to success, what took me years to learn after unlearning everything I'd been taught.

Here it is, friend: Success can only be defined by you. I know I've mentioned it, breadcrumbing it throughout the book, but please hear me on this. In that moment there in the kitchen, I looked around and thought, "I've arrived. I have everything that I need and want, and I will always have an opportunity to create more, but not at the expense of what matters most."

I listened to the promises of what working a little harder looked like. I knew in my mind the work it would take, and I thought to myself, "I could, but then I would have to miss this." I thanked my corporate mentor for thinking of me and let him know that at that particular moment, it wasn't the right goal for me. It was the first time in my direct sales career that I felt in control of my own success.

In life, you can control only your actions, your reactions, and your mindset. For so long I let my goals control me. I let outside influence control me. I let company metrics control me.

As you're reading this, I want to reiterate that I firmly believe working hard isn't an option in direct sales, and there are sacrifices you have to be willing to make. But there is a tragically undiscussed picture that I would like to paint for you: You get to define success. How you choose to build your direct sales business is completely up to you—not your company, not your sponsor, not your mentors, not your team. Success isn't about the end result, it's the process of who you are becoming as you work toward the end result.

For the first part of my direct sales career, I chose to focus on titles and ranks, because that's just what I thought I had to do. After all, it seemed as though everyone achieving those goals was successful, so it had to be the right way to build, right? Working towards those goals was exciting. I'll never forget the first time I walked across the stage, donning medals for the accolades I'd worked so hard to achieve. I didn't get an opportunity like that in my day job. I felt seen and valued by others and by the company. But as the poet Robert Frost so simply stated, "Nothing gold can stay." Nor did the shine and glitz of it stay. It's as if the stage and sparkle were replaced by my messy kitchen and fingerprinted windows.

Never again would I replace the things that mattered most for the things that matter only for a moment.

Defining Success

Okay friend, first, let's remember that success is subjective. In direct sales, that can mean achieving financial stability; for others, it's pursuing personal growth; while others can find success in the titles they earn within the company. Success is really about achieving your goals and feeling a sense of satisfaction, purpose, fulfillment, and accomplishment. In defining success, we want to become aware of how we feel throughout the pursuit of our goals. *Why* we work toward the goal is the cornerstone of success.

In different seasons of my business, I've held different definitions of success. One of my first definitions of success was simply paying for the groceries without breaking the bank. At the time, I was being led by others in the industry who were putting a massive emphasis on accolades in the business and monetary success. Of course, those things piqued my interest, but believing I could achieve those things took time. So I started small by defining success as getting the groceries paid for. While working toward that goal, I was excited! I loved watching our income grow, knowing that I was contributing to our family's success. I loved helping others get excited about the products and learn more about the opportunity. It was a natural high to be serving people what I loved most, and each time I went to the grocery store I was excited knowing that my business was helping us do more than just get by. I was driven by my *why*, enjoying the pursuit, and energized by the achievement.

As my business grew, so did that definition of success. I was still driven by my *why* (contributing to our family's finances in a bigger way), still enjoying the pursuit, and still energized by the achievements. It wasn't until I started feeling removed from my *why* that I saw a rift between my definition of success and the goals that I was working towards.

I was pursuing a huge bonus in my company. It was a lofty goal that meant pushing my team to take action. I was working hard, on calls all the time, working ten to twelve hours a day, and it felt completely out of alignment with my *why*. Although I was still contributing to our family's finances, the pursuit for me was anything but enjoyable. It felt as if someone had sucked the joy out of the process and replaced it with a jackhammer of "hustle, do more, push harder!" And when the goal was achieved, I was zapped. Completely and utterly burnt out.

The key phrase that I want to pause on is "...it felt completely out of alignment with my *why*." There are seasons of the business that require you to sacrifice more, or you may be working toward a goal so you cannot be present with your family as much as you would like. If you need to check yourself to make sure that your goals are aligned with your *why*, ask yourself:

- Do I feel peace in this process?
- Do I like who I am becoming and how I feel in this season?
- Is there an end so that I can pause, take a breath, and reflect on the process?
- Does what I am working on excite me?

For me, the red flags were evident because I didn't feel good about the goal I had set. It wasn't enjoyable and there was no peace through the process. I decided then that working like that wasn't in my best interest. It didn't change my love for the business or the work I did, but it drastically changed my definition of success. I decided to shift the way I was working. Instead of ranks and bonuses, I focused on longevity, depth, and sustainability. When I redefined success, my energy and excitement for the business came back, and my income grew as well.

As you reflect on your own work, your goals, and your personal definition of success, I encourage you to review the following considerations:

- What is the time that you can commit to achieving your goal?
- What is the amount of energy it's going to take to achieve your goal?
- What is the outcome? What is the ROI (time and energy)?
- What are you willing to sacrifice to achieve your goal?
- Who stands to benefit from your definition of success?
- How do you want to feel through the process of achieving success?
- What boundaries need to be put in place to protect your peace?

After realizing that I was pursuing goals that left me completely depleted, I sat down and wrote out my definition of success. I allowed myself to visualize what it would look like to arrive. I shifted my focus away from what everyone else was pursuing and asked myself, "How can this business and this opportunity help me to live a life that *feels* good, without just looking good?" I wrote out the following in my journal:

"I think that success looks a lot like...

- Baking cookies with my kids
- Movie dates with Mike
- Holiday weekends with my family
- Sweating for others when they cannot
- Laughter, lots of laughter
- Making prayer a priority
- Being present
- Being outdoors
- Peace, financially and mindfully
- Making an impact
- Feeling peace with the work I do

Success is working hard, praying hard, and having the courage to hand my worries to God.

Success is not measuring my self-worth by someone else's numbers.

Success is going to bed grateful for the gift of today.

Success is knowing I'm making an impact.

Success is leaning into His calling for me.

Success is working hard but living harder.

And success is being able to put the work away so that my kiddos get the best

SECTION SIX | CHAPTER TWENTY-TWO

of me, not what's left of me. But I assure you my goals are in line with my priorities, even if it's seen as a shortcoming to others."

Reading that journal entry brings tears to my eyes because today—years after writing those words—it is still my definition of success. I am living the life I dreamed of.

My question to you is, are you leaving your definition of success up to someone else, or are you holding the pen and writing it yourself? Here are two more guiding thoughts as you begin to write your own definition of success:

1. Success can only be defined by you. No one has the right to deem whether you feel worthy. You are worthy right where you are, *right now*. You are worthy as you work through the mess of the middle. You are worthy as you venture out into your calling. You are worthy because you are brave enough to venture out and gift others your story.

2. When it gets hard, lean in. Don't walk away from it. Instead, ask yourself, "What can I learn from this hardship? What can I do with this hardship and how can I create a pathway for others who will walk through the same struggles?" Do it for the "well done." Don't give up in the middle of the storm. Get curious about it. And choose to rewrite your definition of success if it's not quite working for you!

Section 6: Takeaways and Final Thoughts

Not too long ago, while I was on a call with my therapist, he said to me, "Katy, I've learned over the years that there are two primary struggles for direct sellers, and selling isn't one of them. It's boundaries and relationships." He nailed it. As you read through these chapters, you likely found yourself wrestling with one or both of those topics. I want to emphasize that you cannot skirt around the hard work that goes into building a direct sales business. There will be sacrifices that need to be made and there will be tough conversations (especially as you grow a team) that need to be had. It isn't easy. Simple? Yes. Easy? No. As your direct sales mentor, I couldn't leave this section untold. Maybe it doesn't apply right now. Who knows? Maybe it never will, but as promised, it's here when you need it.

Key Takeaways:
- Write a list of Healthy CEO qualities and print them out as a reminder of

what matters most.

- Setting boundaries for yourself gives the people around you permission to do the same. Set boundaries so that you can continue to thrive in your work.
- Communicate your goals and your boundaries to those who are most impacted by your work.
- Some people come into your life for a reason, a season, or a lifetime. It's okay to let go of what didn't work out.
- Establish your personal Healthy CEO Rock Solid Routine. Feel free to use mine as a reference.
- Create your Success Statement and honor it.
- Every time you have the urge to compare, replace it with a prayer. Root for her to win and watch as it blesses you in return.

Final Thoughts:

Avoiding my own needs and health almost led me to walk away from a seemingly, on the surface, successful business. Looking back, the signs were so obvious, but at the time I was blinded by my unhealthy business-building habits. I had it all backward.

Today, as a mentor, I see the signs with our clients, and my goal is to help them redirect before they reach the rock bottom I once experienced. Here's what I hope, from the bottom of my heart, that you take from these final chapters:

You can thrive and succeed in your work while giving yourself ample time to rest.

You can make sacrifices for your business that don't cost you your peace of mind.

I teach these things now because I experienced the cost of not honoring those things. Today, as a mentor to thousands in the direct sales and network marketing industry, I can tell you that experiencing real, meaningful, purposeful, peaceful success is possible for you, too.

Friend, you can create success without losing yourself in the process. Remember, there are things that matter and then there are things that *MATTER*. Never sacrifice the things that matter most for the things that matter only for a moment.

Closing Thoughts

"I am a human being, not a human doing."

- KURT VONNEGUT

I don't know much about high jumping, aside from the fact that you hurl yourself over an absurdly high bar after running at a high speed, throwing yourself over the bar only to land on an oversized cushion and then act all cool like nothing ever happened.

However, I am a sucker for a good story, rich in all kinds of analogy, so I'd like to end our time together (or maybe it's the beginning. I hang out on Instagram @ katywritescontent all the time) by sharing a story. It's a story that has stuck with me for years. The first time I shared this story I was standing on stage at a local event after just having missed a large milestone for our company.

I felt like a failure.

I didn't feel worthy of standing on that stage.

I didn't have a shiny new title to put next to my name.

But I did have this story.

What's funny is, looking back at it now, I personally felt like a failure while up on that stage, but something about the story resonated with people. To this day, I still hear from people who were in that audience about the Fosbury Flop.

Let me take you back to the 1968 Summer Olympics. Dick Fosbury, an Olympic high jumper, wasn't happy with his performance leading up to the event. He had been practicing the same technique that those before had used. You see, Fosbury didn't seem like anything special. He was a twenty-one-year-old Civil Engineering major with mismatched shoes. He wasn't a favorite. But at the 1968 Olympics, he changed the sport forever.

If you were to watch the Olympics, his performance wouldn't have seemed like anything special, but those few seconds forever revolutionized the sport. Dick Fosbury was immortalized with his infamous Fosbury Flop. Where every athlete before him had jumped over the bar in a forward motion, scissoring their legs to build additional momentum, Fosbury decided to flop himself, head first, over the bar.

Do you know what blows my mind? Fosbury used his engineering background, knowing that when you arch your back, your center of gravity can stay below the bar, even as you are flying over it.

Well before he made it to the Olympics, he tested his theory over and over again and *flopped* himself forward. His skills weren't so much about his legs, but what was in his head. That day, he set the record, won the gold at 2.24 meters, and created the now-only way to conquer the high jump. At the time, Fosbury's technique was met with skepticism and ridicule from his coaches and fellow athletes. They couldn't understand why he would choose to do things differently, and some even thought he was risking injury with his unorthodox and strange method.

Friend, my point is this: If you want to thrive in direct sales, you must have the courage to flop forward. Like Fosbury, I guarantee you will encounter critics who don't understand your business. Like Fosbury, you will likely attempt to go about business in the same way as others, only to find that it doesn't work for you. (Did I mention that Fosbury, shortly before becoming an Olympic athlete, lost a bet to jump over a chair, breaking his hand in the process? But I digress…) I guarantee, and I am sorry to say, that many times you will feel like you're flying, only to realize you're flopping.

But here's what I want you to know—and this is the part I love about Fosbury that I want for you too—don't get caught up in all of it, you know? Fosbury missed the opening ceremonies. He was off exploring the pyramids and sleeping in a van, living what he believed to be the good life during the 1968 Olympics. Just, you know, YOLO #livinghisbestlife? So, I have a piece of advice that I'd love for you to tuck into your back pocket, advice that I would've loved (even if I didn't listen to it): Don't get caught up in it all. There is so much opportunity in direct sales, lots of bells and whistles, and perks and incentives. Don't worry about the accolades and recognition. Don't worry about the titles and what everyone else around you is earning. Sure, those things are fun, a nice perk of the work you're doing, and worth working toward. But in the words of my man Robert Frost, "Nothing gold can stay."

Guys, it pains me to admit this. I know firsthand through my personal health battles that the time we have here is so precious, and I spent a lot of time unknowingly taking that for granted.

I can never get back the time I chose to chase goals that didn't align with my values, but…

I can share my experience. I can share the part that I'm least proud of.

I can share the nights I chose my computer over my husband.

I can share the nights I rushed my kids to bed so I could work.

And I can share what I live out now: Success, the simple kind, can be achieved without losing sight of what matters most.

I've learned, through a lot of untangling and unlearning, how to become a Healthy CEO, a truly simple, intentional, and joyful CEO.

So, here's what I'd advise, looking back on eleven years of highs and lows and lessons learned. Focus on the impact that you are making. Focus on the way your business is positively impacting those around you. Focus on how to serve well. Focus on who you are becoming through the process of building a business. Remember, that there are things that matter, and there are things that *MATTER*. Never sacrifice the things that matter most for the things that matter only for a moment.

In the process of achieving the goals, the titles, and the accolades, may you never forget what you set out to achieve in the first place. There is nothing more that I want for you than to create a business that you love, a business you are proud of, and a business that FEELS good and blesses others.

It's my hope that you move forward, hopefully with lots of highlights and notes and sticky tabs, knowing that you never have to go it alone. Be grateful for every ungraceful flop you experience, because every flop is actually how you move forward. You can do *Direct Sales Done Right*, and in case you ever forget, I am rooting for you.

-Katy

ABOUT THE AUTHOR

Katy Ursta is the co-CEO of Chic Influencer, an online digital content company, as well as an eleven-year veteran of the direct sales industry. She is the co-author of The Direct Sales Done Right 52 Week Social Media Planner and the author of the Back Pocket Prayer Journal. Her personal writings have been featured on sites such as Scary Mommy, Her View From Home, and The Today Show. When she isn't behind the computer screen helping women maximize their potential, she's likely at the hockey rink, cheering on her two sons, Nick and Dom.

She believes every story matters and has helped thousands of aspiring direct sellers succeed by teaching them to pursue their unique vision for their own businesses.

Come Say Hi!
IG @katywriescontent
FB Katy Ursta
Chicinfluencer.com

ACKNOWLEDGEMENTS

One of my personal Back Pocket Prayers that I found myself repeating throughout the process of writing and editing this book was:

"Lord, *soften* my edges but *sharpen* my words so that I may do your work through my words."

As I wrote this book, I found myself reflecting deeply on my personal direct sales experience—the less-than-polished moments, the indescribable bigger-than-me moments, and so many of the gritty, seemingly insignificant moments in between. I am so grateful for all of these moments because they've shaped me into the person I am now: the Christian, the writer, the coach, the mom, the wife, the friend—a woman I never would've had the courage to become without the lessons learned through this opportunity.

I am thankful especially for the team of women at Chic Influencer, and my personal direct sales sponsor who introduced me to the world of network marketing, Melanie. I am grateful for my editor, Margaret, who encouraged me throughout the writing and editing process to confidently continue to Drive Toward Daylight.

I am thankful for all the women and men I've learned from throughout each season of my business. I am thankful for every one of them (some with whom I worked for only a season, some for a reason, and some who I'm blessed to have for a lifetime).

I thank every customer, every distributor, everyone who told me "no," and everyone who said, "yes." I thank every mentor who paved the way with their best practices and their humbling mistakes. I thank every single person who ever encouraged me with a word, with a social media "like," with a nudge to keep writing or keep sweating, but most importantly to just keep going.

And to bring it back to where it all began, to *why* it all began: Thank you to my boys, Mike, Nick, and Dom.

Keep Driving Toward Daylight.

Rooting for you, always,
Katy

WORKS CITED

Staff, DSJ. "Attitudes toward Direct Selling: How Entrepreneurs and Consumers See the Channel." *Direct Selling Journal - A DSA Publication*, 17 May 2022, www.dsa.org/direct-selling-journal/direct-selling-journal-latest-articles/attitudes-toward-direct-selling-how-entrepreneurs-and-consumers-see-the-channel.

Brianna Wiest, *101 Essays That Will Change the Way You Think*, ebook edition, (Thought Catalogs Books, 2017).

Haley Goldberg, "The One Question I Ask To Stop Negative Thoughts From Ruining My Day," *Fast Company*, July 28, 2017, https://www.fastcompany.com/40444942/the-one-question-i-ask-myself-to-stop-negative-thoughts-from-ruining-my-day

Margarita Tartakovsky, MS, "How and When to Say No," *Psych Central*, June 14, 2021, https://psychcentral.com/lib/learning-to-say-no

Jason Falls, *Winfluence: Reframing Influencer Marketing to Ignite Your Brand*, ebook edition, (Entrepreneur Press, 2021).

Donald Miller, introduction to *Building a StoryBrand: Clarify Your Message So Customers Will Listen*, epub edition (Harper Collins Leadership, 2017), ix.

Niki Hall, "Four Core Elements Of Building A Trusted Brand," *Forbes*, July 1, 2022, https://www.forbes.com/sites/forbescommunicationscouncil/2022/07/01/four-core-elements-of-building-a-trusted-brand/

Jeff Henderson, *Know What You're FOR*, ebook edition, (Zondervan, 2019).

Robert Cialdini, *Influence: The Psychology of Persausion*, ebook edition, (Harper Collins, 2007).

Nusair Bawla, "Sales Persistence Pays Off," *Business News Daily*, February 21, 2023, https://www.businessnewsdaily.com/5389-in-sales-persistence-pays-off.html

"149 Eye-Opening Sales Statistics to Consider in 2023 (By Category)," *Spotio*, January 20, 2023, https://spotio.com/blog/sales-statistics/

WORKS CITED

Joyce Meyer, *Battlefield of the Mind*, Faith Words edition, (Hatchette Book Group, Inc., 2011).

Robert C. Pozen, "Exercise Increases Productivity," *Brookings*, October 24, 2012, https://www.brookings.edu/articles/exercise-increases-productivity/